DATE DUE			
FEB 1 3 '85			
FEB 17			
OCT 0 6 1987			

Lyndon Johnson and the Southern Military Tradition

J. Michael Quill

University Press of America™

Copyright © 1977 by

University Press of America™

division of
R.F. Publishing, Inc.
4710 Auth Place, S.E., Washington, D.C. 20023

I SBN 0–8191–0354–3

"A president's hardest task is not
to do what is right, but to know
what is right. Yet the presidency
brings no special gift of prophecy
or foresight. You take an oath,
step into an office, and must help
guide a great democracy. The answer
was waiting for me in the land where
I was born."--Lyndon B. Johnson

TO

CLARA SNIVELY QUILL,

WIFE AND FRIEND

PREFACE

This writer is convinced that the year 1963 marked a
critical turning point in the course of American history. It
is perhaps not terribly intrepid to predict that future generations gazing back at our times might very well label the decade
of the 1960's "the Age of Vietnam." Believing this to be the
case, this author has ventured slightly out of his area of
alleged specialization to investigate some of the possible
reasons why the conflict in Southeast Asia changed so
drastically in scope after 1963. Because in that year, while
there was indeed an American presence in the war, the commitment of military personnel to South Vietnam was still of rather
modest proportions. Yet, the years following would witness
one increase and escalation after another, until eventually
one half million Americans would be serving there by 1967.
The key to this significant modification in the nature of the
war was the character and personality of President Lyndon
Baines Johnson.

This is not a book by an "insider," rather it is the work
of an historian who never had the opportunity of even meeting
that Chief Executive. Neither is it a biography of Lyndon
Johnson, at least not in the strict sense of that term. Nor
is it a complete or comprehensive history of the Vietnam War.
Rather, it combines elements of biography, the progress of the
war, and the influence of Johnson's Southern background to
hopefully present a fuller picture of some of the powerful
forces operating upon the President from Texas. While a careful effort was made to go through President Johnson's memoirs
and public papers, this study is primarily a work of synthesis,
resting heavily and unashamedly upon the many and perceptive
secondary sources covering various aspects of this subject.

The organization of the work is in most instances topical.
The opening chapter traces the origins of the Vietnam involvement from roughly the start of World War II down to the assassination of John F. Kennedy. Chapter Two then looks at Lyndon
Johnson's massive buildup of the war effort, while the next
chapter attempts to offer some explanations for his actions.
Reaching the conclusion that one of the most important elements
in Johnson's outlook was his Southern heritage, Chapter Four
surveys the unique and distinctive experience of the South,
especially concentrating upon the violent and militant aspects
of the Southland's past. And finally, the last chapter tries

to present Johnson as typically Southern in many facets of his character, with special attention given to his infatuation with things military.

* * * * *

The author owes a special debt of gratitude to many persons in many places. This study began as a seminar paper while the writer was in graduate school, and then was laid aside for several years. The director of that seminar, Dr. Vincent P. DeSantis of the University of Notre Dame, has my special thanks for encouraging me to complete the work, and his kindness and consideration have always been an inspiration. Similarly, anyone pursuing the study of history soon discovers how critically dependent our craft is upon the assistance and goodwill of librarians, and in this regard I have indeed been fortunate. I want to extend special thanks to Sister Frances Claire Mezera and Sister Nona Grover of the Viterbo College library, to Mrs. Helen Leide and the many other dedicated members of the staff at the Murphy Library of the University of Wisconsin--La Crosse, and to the always helpful personnel of the University of Notre Dame's Memorial Library. Also, I would like to express special appreciation to Elizabeth Kindschy who very expertly typed and assisted me at many points with the final preparation of the manuscript. And finally, as usual, I owe my greatest debt to my wife Clara Snively Quill. She was very generous in sharing with me her thoughts and insights, and all the while understandingly tolerated the author's crotchets. Needless to say, all errors are mine alone.

J. M. Q.

iv

INTRODUCTION

"It has been my greatest desire, since assuming this office, to be a President of peace."[1] These words were spoken by the thirty-sixth President of the United States, Lyndon Baines Johnson, a man who desired peace but who presided over war. He dreamed of a "Great Society," but found instead a society turbulently rent by a controversial war in a strange and faraway land. He exuded pride over America's military establishment, but saw the military, and himself, increasingly criticized and maligned during his Administration. In 1964 Lyndon Johnson was elected to the presidency by an almost unprecedented majority, but in 1968 he chose not to be a candidate for that office. These were the troublesome pieces in a mosaic of pain and frustration which would form the basis for the tragedy of Lyndon Johnson.

To understand the events leading to the downfall of that exuberant and proud man from Texas, it is necessary to ascertain that President's relationship with the military. It is the military which fights wars, and it was a war that spoiled Johnson's dreams. It was Lyndon Johnson's attitudes toward the military and its role in world affairs which set the stage for the tragedy. It was these firmly held opinions which prevented Johnson from extricating himself from a position which was rapidly growing unpopular and untenable. His failure to abandon a politically ruinous course was in large part due to certain deeply ingrained beliefs, and this failure would bring on the denouement of the debacle. It is within this context that an understanding of Johnson's military attitudes is essential.

* * * * *

At the time of John Kennedy's death and Johnson's acession to the Presidency, relations between the Pentagon military establishment and the Defense Department civilian experts were badly strained. Kennedy had been increasingly reluctant to listen very much to the generals and admirals in the aftermath

1

of the Bay of Pigs fiasco, and they fared poorly in their attempts to appeal Secretary of Defense McNamara's decisions to him.[2] One associate of the late President observed at the time that one didn't "see much of the Joint Chiefs around the White House any more".[3] McNamara had especially angered Admiral George W. Anderson, then Chief of Naval Operations and a member of the Joint Chiefs of Staff. Anderson had been at odds with the Defense Department civilians on several issues, but the real break came when McNamara scuttled the plans for a nuclear-powered aircraft carrier.[4] The Admiral soon discovered, however, that Kennedy's loyalties lay with McNamara, and in the end Anderson was eased out of the Pentagon through an appointment as Ambassador to Portugal. But before Admiral Anderson departed, he fired a fusillade at the civilian experts of the Defense Department.[5]

In a speech on September 4, 1963, at Washington's National Press Club, Anderson stated that certain aspects of the Department of Defense gave him, and many others in uniform, great anxiety. He told his audience:

> I am gravely concerned that within the Department of Defense there is not the degree of confidence and trust between the civilian and military echelons that the importance of their common objective requires... The recommendations of the uniformed chiefs of our services, each backed up by competent military and civilian staffs, are altered or overruled without interim consultation, explanation and discussion...[6]

The Admiral concluded his remarks with the warning that such ignoring of military recommendations "is fraught...potentially with grave dangers."[7]

This distress and dismay over the waning of military influence in the Kennedy Administration was by no means confined to the generals and admirals. Writers and journalists from the right end of the political spectrum were also concerned, and were quick to express their forebodings. The conservative analyst Frank L. Kluckhohn, in a book purporting to present a "candid look at the President's policymakers," entitled one of his chapters "The Amateur Strategists vs. the Joint Chiefs." He was denouncing such policy makers as Dean Rusk, Walt Rostow, George Ball, Harlan Cleveland, Adam Yarmolinsky, Robert S. McNamara, Paul H. Nitze, Jerome Wiesner, McGeorge Bundy, and Arthur M. Schlesinger, Jr.[8] Kluckhohn wrote: "Today our military establishment is under control of the Administration's civilian Inner Circle. The Joint Chiefs of Staff have been subordinated."[9] And the syndicated newspaper columnist Ralph de Toledano revealed to his readers that "morale in the armed forces is lower today than it has ever been...the civilians

brought in by Secretary McNamara have shut off debate--like the
Napoleon who became intolerant of criticism, stifled his commanders, and ended his great career in utter defeat."[10]

Implicit in these lamentations of the Pentagon military
chiefs and the conservative press was the hope that a different
President would reverse the policy of benign neglect toward the
military brass and lessen the tyranny of the civilian experts
over the Joint Chiefs. In fact, Kluckhohn even entitled his
book Lyndon's Legacy, implying that the new President could be-
queath a legacy of inestimable value to the nation if he would
determine to accord the proper respect to his military advisers
and be attentive to their needs and counsel. At least one
conservative observer, however, was not at all certain that
Lyndon Johnson could be counted on for any such determined
course of action. J. Evetts Haley, in a bitterly critical book
about the President, badly underestimated LBJ's tenacity when
he declared: "There is nothing more significant in Johnson's
career than the fact that he has never been known to take an
unpopular position and resolutely go down the line for it."[11]

In retrospect, these fears and doubts about the declining
role of the military advisers late in 1963 now have a ring of
cruel irony. Even the most optimistic proponent of military
influence in government could scarcely have predicted the degree
to which the new President would become dependent upon the
military; and the most prescient of analysts would have found
it hard to believe that the same Chief Executive would soon
engage the country in its longest war and its most bitter
national policy debate since the days of the Civil War. Far
from ignoring the military, Lyndon Johnson could publicly proclaim in August of 1964 a high degree of confidence and cooperation between the military and his Administration. On that occasion the President remarked: "I want the whole world to know
that in this land there is today a strong mutual confidence
between military men and civilian political leaders. This is
true at every level."[12] Once again employing the historian's
prerogative of hindsight, it would appear that one of the more
perceptive statements concerning the new President's future
course was made almost inadvertently, in a very friendly
biography written by Henry Zeiger. In his 1963 assessment of
LBJ, Zeiger astutely noted the following: "On some matters,
however, Johnson's position is unequivocal. He has always
been interested in defense matters, and he has always urged
the country to be militarily strong. He has always supported
a buildup of our armed forces...."[13] And Jack Bell, writing in
1965, came much closer to the real significance and import of
any Johnson legacy when he observed: "As he marched down the
corridors of the years ahead of him it would be Lyndon Baines
Johnson's destiny to preside over a peaceful reorganization of
the world's power structure or over the dissolution of civili-

3

zation. This was the rendezvous with history of the man from
Texas."[14] And this rendezvous with history for President
Lyndon Johnson would take place in an obscure and even unlikely
spot, a little country nestled in the teeming jungles of Southeast Asia--Vietnam.

INTRODUCTION

FOOTNOTES

[1] U. S., National Archives and Records Service, Public Papers of the Presidents of the United States: Lyndon B. Johnson, VI, Doc. 377, August 11, 1966, 816.

[2] Jack Bell, The Johnson Treatment: How Lyndon B. Johnson Took Over the Presidency and Made It His Own (New York, 1965), p. 182.

[3] Quoted in Ibid.

[4] Frank L. Kluckhohn, Lyndon's Legacy: A Candid Look at the President's Policymakers (New York, 1964), p. 114.

[5] Bell, The Johnson Treatment, p. 182.

[6] Quoted in Kluckhohn, Lyndon's Legacy, p. 114.

[7] Quoted in Ibid.

[8] Ibid., p. 126.

[9] Quoted in Ibid.

[10] Quoted in Ibid., p. 115.

[11] J. Evetts Haley, A Texan Looks at Lyndon: A Study in Illegitimate Power (Canyon, Texas, 1964), p. 172.

[12] Public Papers, II, Doc. 533, August 21, 1964, 1001.

[13] Henry A. Zeiger, Lyndon B. Johnson: Man and President (New York, 1963), p. 106.

[14] Bell, The Johnson Treatment, p. 294.

CHAPTER I

THE ORIGINS OF THE VIETNAM WAR, 1940-1963

Lyndon Johnson did not start the Vietnam War. To be sure, he escalated that conflict far beyond any previous level and engendered a divisiveness in the country infinitely greater than that incurred by any of his immediate predecessors, for reasons that will be investigated later in this study. But the fact remains that the war in Vietnam was conceived and instigated initially by other American Presidents in other times. Whatever the verdict of history on what later became known as "Mr. Johnson's War," it must be kept in mind that it was a second or third-hand affair for the President from Texas, an inherited war. Johnson was quite right when he pointed out, in the midst of the 1964 campaign, that: "I didn't get you into Vietnam. You have been in Vietnam 10 years."[1]

If anything, Johnson minimized the length of American interest and involvement with the destiny and fortunes of Vietnam. The American experience with Vietnam extended back much farther than most Americans generally realized. Indeed, it can be cogently argued that Vietnam loomed large in the series of events which brought the United States into World War II. Because it was that area, then called French Indochina, that the Japanese began occupying in the middle of 1940.[2] These Japanese advances were not strongly resisted by the French, who were hampered by a serious lack of resources.[3] By 1941 Franklin Roosevelt was convinced that the Japanese inroads into Indochina posed a dangerous threat to American interests in that region. Roosevelt perceived that a successful Japanese occupation of Vietnam would permit Tokyo a jumping-off point for a more extended aggression against all of Southeast Asia. In addition, the American defense effort was greatly dependent upon an unmolested flow of natural rubber from the area, and any occupation there by Japan would seriously jeopardize that flow. Therefore, when the Japanese made more demands on Indochina in July of 1941 it set off a chain reaction whereby the American government decided to freeze all Japanese assets in the United States, and this, in turn, was a powerful motive in the decision of Japan to bomb the American fleet stationed at Pearl Harbor.[4]

But even after precipitating American entry into the Second World War, Vietnam still troubled the mind of President

Roosevelt. Roosevelt perceived that the war would probably in-
spire a revolt against European colonialism on a world scale.
FDR was convinced that Indochina was one of the weakest bastions
of the western colonial empire. So in March of 1943 he proposed
to Anthony Eden, the British Foreign Minister, that Indochina
should not be restored to France following the war, but instead,
it should be made an international trusteeship nation. It was
Roosevelt's hope that Indochina could then be prepared for
independence. The President discussed his plan with Allied war
leaders, including Chiang Kai-shek and Stalin, but Roosevelt
died before his idea could become reality. Shortly after his
death the State Department issued a statement to the effect
that there could not be any trusteeship in Indochina unless it
were under French auspices.[5]

Then, just five months following the death of Roosevelt, a
Vietnamese Communist named Ho Chi Minh issued the Declaration of
Independence of the Democratic Republic of Vietnam. Ho Chi Minh
had been associated with the Comintern for a period of twenty
years, and had later arisen as a leader in the resistance movement against the Japanese. In this latter capacity he had
cooperated closely with the American Office of Strategic
Services. The exact amount of aid given to Ho Chi Minh's forces
the Viet Minh, by the OSS is not precisely known. Most likely
it was not extremely large; but the psychological effect was
much greater. Because the OSS aid enabled Ho Chi Minh to claim
that the Viet Minh were really part of the Allied war effort
against Japan. He could also claim that his forces had American
support during their initial attempts to win Vietnamese independence. Whatever the actual amount of the aid, however, there
were OSS officers leading and training Ho's guerrilla army
during the closing months of the war.[6]

The French response to all this was a stubborn determinatio
to restore Indochina to its proper place in the old scheme of
colonial rule. This attempt by France to reassert its empire
in the region precipitated eight years of bitter and savage
conflict between the French, along with some Vietnamese allies,
and the Viet Minh forces of Ho Chi Minh. The war's end had
generated a powerful force of nationalism in Vietnam, and being
the most aggressive of the national resistence forces, the Viet
Minh were able to garner widespread support and allegiance all
over the country. Ho Chi Minh was now beginning to emerge more
and more as a national hero in Vietnam's struggle for independence.[7]

At the outset of the fighting, American officials gave the
whole affair very little of their attention or consideration.
If anything, American sympathies were with the Vietnamese
nationalists in the first several weeks of that conflict which
followed in the wake of Japan's surrender.[8] The Truman

Administration refused to yield to the French requests for American planes or ships to transport French fighting men to Indochina, and he also decided against supplying any American arms for the war against the Viet Minh. But if Truman snubbed the French entreaties for assistance, he similarly rebuffed Ho Chi Minh's appeals. In August and September of 1945, Ho's army was in control of Hanoi. It was at this juncture that the guerrilla leader contacted President Truman by means of the Office of Strategic Services. Ho was asking that a period of American guardianship be provided for Vietnam while it prepared for independence, an arrangement similar to what had been established for the Philippines. The secret Pentagon study on the origins of the Vietnam War reveals that Ho forwarded at least eight letters to President Truman in the interval between October of 1945 and February of the following year. He was seeking intervention by the United States or the United Nations against French colonialism. It is highly unlikely that any of these appeals were ever answered.[9]

If there ever was a chance for an American protectorship in cooperation with Ho Chi Minh, these hopes were quickly dissipated by the disconcerting events of the early Cold War period. Throughout 1948 and 1949 the United States was greatly concerned about Soviet expansion in Eastern Europe, and the Communist affiliations of Ho Chi Minh now made him suspect in the eyes of many American officials. Then following in rapid succession came, in 1949, the fall of mainland China to the Chinese Communist forces of Mao Tse-tung and, in 1950, the invasion of South Korea by North Korean Communist armies. At this point all American indifference, neutrality, and ambivalence in regard to Vietnam ended, quickly and dramatically. In the light of those events, it now appeared to the American government that the French were plugging the dyke against further communism in Asia. So a crucial corner was turned in the winter of 1949-50, because it was then that the United States made a momentous decision which would help determine the course of American policy in Vietnam for the next twenty years. It so happened that after the loss of China, the Truman Administration then promised to grant military assistance to the French forces against the Communist-led Viet Minh and assured support for the French client regime in Saigon under Emperor Bao Dai. Of course, these decisions were made in the midst of sudden and shocking events in Eastern Europe and Asia, but they had the effect of easing the American government's qualms about becoming entangled with French colonialism in Indochina, too. So now Washington was prepared to make the necessary efforts to halt further Communist aggrandizement in Asia.[10] And, as the Pentagon study points out, "the United States thereafter was directly involved in the developing tragedy in Vietnam."[11]

8

And the Truman Administration matched words with actions. On May 8, 1950, Washington made good on its promise of economic and military aid to the French in Indochina with a grant of ten million dollars. But this was only a beginning. The Eisenhower Administration, if anything, enlarged upon Truman's policy. In fact, between Truman's initial grant in 1950 and the cessation of hostilities in the spring of 1954, the United States allocated to the French about $2.6 billion in war material. This amounted to almost 80 percent of the entire French cost of the war.[12]

* * * * *

It was during the Eisenhower years that the possibility of employing American troops in Vietnam was discussed seriously for the first time. Eisenhower's Secretary of State, John Foster Dulles, was taking a strong stand on the issue of communism in that region of Asia. Dulles was worried about the looming threat of the Chinese, and warned in September of 1953 that "as in Korea, Red China might send its own army into Indochina...." And it was not long until merely the specter of a Viet Minh victory, even without any involvement by the Red Chinese, was alarming the Administration. President Eisenhower told a press conference early in 1954 that there was "a row of dominoes set up," and if the first one were to be knocked over, "what will happen to the last one is that it will go over quickly." This was the birth of the so-called "domino theory" into the national nomenclature.[13]

The real crisis occurred during mid-April of 1954 when the Viet Minh besieged the French fortress of Dienbienphu. With the fate of that French stronghold hanging in the balance, the commander there asked for military assistance from the United States. Several officials in the Eisenhower Administration used strong and bellicose language in assessing the alternatives. The chairman of the Joint Chiefs of Staff, Admiral Radford, opted for an air strike originating in the Philippines. Vice President Nixon went on record as perhaps even being in favor of "putting our boys in." This kind of talk even generated some rumors to the effect that bombing, perhaps the Atomic Bomb, might be used in order to relieve the French garrison. However, there is scanty evidence of any such notion being seriously considered by the President. President Eisenhower was dubious about the feasibility of any kind of unilateral military intervention on the part of the United States, and so he decided to try for British collaboration. But the British were not interested, fearing that a military operation would be ineffective, and might lead the world to the brink of a major war.[14]

The hints and rumors about the possibility of American intervention caused some ripples of consternation in Washington, too. General Matthew Ridgway, who had been the commander of the

9

United Nations effort in Korea and who was presently serving as Army Chief of Staff, was critical of the idea of any bombing or sending of American men to fight a war in Asia. He regarded any such plan as strategically indefensible. Ridgway's views were also shared by General James Gavin, who was Chief of Plans. It is interesting to note, too, that a number of senators expressed doubts and reservations on this issue of American involvement. Included in this group, ironically enough, were John F. Kennedy and Lyndon B. Johnson.[15]

Thus, ultimately, the opposition of congressional leaders, of Generals Ridgway and Gavin, and of the British caused the administration to set aside its ideas for a military intervention.[16] However, as the Pentagon study points out, "the public has not understood how seriously the Eisenhower Administration debated intervention." The Pentagon Papers reveal that during May and June of 1954 Eisenhower went so far as to have some of his aides draw up a resolution which asked for the Congress's authority to commit American troops in Indochina.[17]

Following President Eisenhower's decision not to intervene, Dienbienphu did fall to the Viet Minh and France abandoned the fight in Indochina. Peace negotiations were then held at Geneva, but the United States refused to be a participant in them. The upshot of the Geneva Conference was a de facto partition for Vietnam, the line to be drawn at the 17th parallel. The accords also guaranteed the independence of Laos and Cambodia.[18] Then, just two months later, Secretary Dulles attended a conference at Manila, and it was at this meeting that the Southeast Asia Treaty Organization (SEATO) was established. The nations signing this pact, in addition to the United States, included Pakistan, Thailand, the Philippines, Australia, New Zealand, France, and Great Britain. A special element of the Treaty was a protocol adding South Vietnam, Laos, and Cambodia to the areas which were to be covered and protected by the new organization. The primary result of the Manila Conference was to involve the United States deeply in Southeast Asian affairs.[19]

On the other hand, the agreements reached at Geneva did not work out well at all. The secret Pentagon study notes that the Eisenhower Administration's National Security Council came to the conclusion that the agreements were disastrous and that efforts had to be made to block any renewed Communist expansion in Vietnam. This disclosure weakens the arguments of several American Administrations that the North Vietnamese alone were responsible for undermining the provisions of the Geneva accords. The Pentagon assessment concludes that the United States had "a direct role in the ultimate breakdown of the Geneva settlement."[20] On August 3, 1954, the National Security Council recommended an immediate program of economic and military aid to the new South Vietnamese Government of Ngo Dinh Diem, then

Premier and later President. This, in effect, would replace French advisers with American advisers. The Council's objectives were to support a friendly non-Communist government in South Vietnam and to avoid a Communist victory through the country-wide elections provided for at Geneva.[21]

In relation to supporting South Vietnam, President Eisenhower took a fateful step when he responded, in a letter, to Ngo Dinh Diem's request for economic assistance. In his letter, Eisenhower promised American support "to assist the Government of Viet Nam in developing and maintaining a strong, viable state, capable of resisting attempted subversion or aggression through military means." The American President added, however, that ideally this aid should be in conjunction with "performance on the part of the Government of Viet-Nam in undertaking needed reforms."[22] This Eisenhower letter was the culmination of many weeks of review and analysis. The President finally became convinced that American support would be essential for the continued existence of a free South Vietnam.[23]

Meanwhile, in South Vietnam, Ngo Dinh Diem authorized a referendum vote which would allow citizens to choose between himself and Bao Dai. The outcome of the referendum was never really in doubt, with Diem collecting a resounding total of 98.2 percent of the vote. Following this electoral landslide, Premier Diem then proclaimed himself President. However, the new President was less than enthusiastic about certain other elections. By the provisions agreed upon at the Geneva Conference, the two sections of Vietnam were to enter into consultation in July, 1955 to discuss the national elections which were scheduled for the next year. But Diem realized that his North Vietnamese rival, Ho Chi Minh, would fare extremely well in any such all-Vietnamese elections, so he refused to participate in any talks with the Communists. Thus, in July of 1956 Diem decided not to hold the elections for reunification. The South Vietnamese leader argued that his government had not signed the Geneva accords and therefore was not bound by them.[24]

Also realizing the electoral strength of Ho Chi Minh, the Eisenhower Administration backed up Saigon in its resolve not to honor the elections provision in the Geneva agreements.[25] The Pentagon Papers make it clear that the United States was not guilty of conniving with Diem to ignore the elections, since documents in the State Department demonstrate that Diem's actions were of his own volition. Yet, the Pentagon study also marshals evidence from State Department cables, and from memorandums of the National Security Council, which show that the Eisenhower Administration plainly wanted to postpone the elections indefinitely, and that such wishes were communicated to Mr. Diem.[26]

Be this as it may, the Saigon regime received much more than American wishes. The prevailing assumption in Washington was that significant amounts of American economic and political support would be required to guarantee the existence of South Vietnam as a free and independent state. The American government earmarked $2.3 billion of aid--three-fifths economic and two-fifths military--for South Vietnam during the next five years. And for a brief period at least, it seemed as if the money was well spent. South Vietnam's rice and sugar production went up, as did the production of textiles. There was also progress evident in the construction of schools and medical facilities, as well as a program of rudimentary land reform. And certainly not least important was the fact that American military advisers were laying the foundations for a South Vietnamese army.[27]

Nevertheless, beneath the surface, things were not proceeding so well. President Diem was a typical example of the older generation of nationalists in Vietnam, who tended to be of the upper class, and who were French speaking and Catholic. Diem had come out of a family which was both staunchly Roman Catholic and a part of the traditional Mandarin ruling class. He had been a diligent and devoted supporter of national independence, yet he wanted to accomplish that goal without upsetting the classical structure and hierarchy of Vietnamese society.[28] The demeanor of Ngo Dinh Diem was at once authoritarian, moralistic, inflexible, bureaucratic, and suspicious. In the Pentagon study his mentality is described as resembling that of a "Spanish Inquisitor."[29] True to his background, Diem was able to subdue the various religious groups, brought about a cleaning up of Saigon, and attempted to bring back the old Annamese morality. Personally a man of rectitude, devotion, and integrity, he nevertheless found it impossible to identify with the aspirations of the masses, aspirations which had been enkindled by the fight for independence. Diem was the complete traditionalist; to his way of thinking the duty of the common people was to respect and faithfully follow the orders of their leaders. Really the Diem regime was an oriental family despotism. For instance, elected village government was abolished in 1956, with the result that more and more power now accrued to the president and his brothers.[30]

His regime disregarded much of the heritage of western democracy, too, with any opposition being equated with disloyalty. Diem's rule included manhunts, camps for political reeducation, and in some cases, population regroupment. Not surprisingly, tactics like these gave rise to serious discontent and even some armed resistance in the countryside. These guerrilla groups operating within South Vietnam itself were called the Viet Cong. By 1958 the civil rebellion in Diem's country was beginning to pick up momentum, and in September of 1960 the Communist Party of North Vietnam welcomed the Viet Cong into its fold. At the same time the North Vietnamese government proclaimed the need for a liberation of the south from the grasping tenacles of American imperialism. It was at this stage that Ho Chi Minh began aiding the Viet Cong forces in terms of training, equipment, strategic planning, and even manpower. By 1960 there were perhaps two thousand North Vietnamese soldiers a year who headed south to join ranks with the Viet Cong.[31]

Back in Saigon, Diem was usually able to follow his authoritarian inclinations without very many American objections. Compared to the chaos existing in other ex-colonial areas in Asia and Africa, and in Latin America, South Vietnam and Diem did not come off too badly.[32] Yet, before 1960 ended the guerrillas in the south were making larger and bolder attacks. Likewise, the Communist rebels in Laos--the Pathet Lao--were having a great deal of success, and this facilitated the transporting of assistance from North Vietnam into the south. In addition, the American military advisers had taught the South Vietnamese army to fight a more conventional style of warfare, and so that army was proving to be more and more ineffective. Perhaps as many as 15,000 Viet Cong were now overrunning large areas of South Vietnam, by both day and night. And in Saigon, Diem's autocratic ways, as well as his methods of waging the war, were drawing increasing amounts of opposition and criticism. A dangerous portion of the discontent was centered in the army, and a military coup almost succeeded in unseating the Diem government in November of 1960. But after putting down this coup, Diem became even more authoritarian and less receptive to any variety of opposition. Feeling now that he could trust no one, he withdrew increasingly into his family, and relied heavily on his brother, Ngo Dinh Nhu.[33] This was the situation which confronted the new American President elected in that November of 1960--John F. Kennedy.

* * * * *

John F. Kennedy entered the White House with idealism, enthusiasm, and high moral purpose. The new President and his team were imbued with an exciting sense of American elitism. They were confident that the very best and brightest had been summoned to bring the American dream to fruition. These men were dedicated to the tantilizing vista of a fresh and dynamic American nationalism. A new nationalism which would add a vigorous and impelling spirit to America's historic role in the affairs of the world. In many respects it would seem like an attempt to realize the American dream not only at home, but elsewhere in the world as well. It involved a redefinition of what comprised American aspirations, and then infusing those

traditional aspirations with a youthful and vernal sense of
purpose. This was the opportunity to reshape American life,
which had perhaps grown somewhat materialistic and complacent,
by instilling into it a grand new crusade and mission.[34] These
lofty hopes and high expectations were given eloquent, if
somewhat scary, expression in Kennedy's Inaugural Address:
"Let every nation know, whether it wishes us well or ill, that
we shall pay any price, bear any burden, meet any hardship,
support any friend, oppose any foe, in order to assure the
survival and success of liberty. This much we pledge--and more."
Implicit in such words was a conviction that the country was
confronting a rival and hostile power bloc which was bent upon
world conquest. In other words, the United States must be
vigilant, and must be prepared to contend with those foes and
to defend the interests of the nation in an unfriendly world.[35]

So it was in January of 1961 that the dead weight of the
Vietnam quagmire descended upon this young President. At key
points during the preceding years the Administrations of Truman
and Eisenhower had made little-noticed yet far-reaching decisions concerning the nation's Vietnam policy. By the time
John Kennedy assumed the Presidency, the American government
felt itself firmly entrusted with the defense of South Vietnam.[36]
Kennedy had believed for some time that the primary communist
tactic for the future would be neither nuclear nor conventional
war, but rather, conflicts waged according to the maxims of
guerrilla fighting. Therefore, it seemed to the new Chief
Executive that the best means of dealing with the Viet Cong
menace would be through just such jungle tactics, or the term
which was in vogue during the Kennedy years, "counterinsurgency."[37]

A crucial development for the Kennedy Administration came
in October of 1961 when the President dispatched General Maxwell
Taylor and Walt W. Rostow, a White House aide, on a special
fact-finding tour to Saigon. The result was the famous Taylor-
Rostow Report. This very important document recommended to
Kennedy the need for an increase in the American role. According to the report, this enlargement would come mainly
through the addition of American "advisers" to the South
Vietnamese army (ARVN) and to the government. Taylor and
Rostow likewise suggested that an American military task force
of eight or ten thousand men should perhaps be sent to Vietnam,
where they could handle defensive operations or, in an
emergency, be put into action as reserves. The two observers
made it clear that the success of their proposal was predicated
upon the stopping of enemy infiltration from the north. However, if this infiltration did not cease, the report recommended
a policy of retaliation directed against the north, the reprisals to match the intensity and extent of northern aid.[38]

This Taylor-Rostow mission greatly altered and escalated
the American commitment to Vietnam. Although Kennedy decided
against both the northern strategy and the deployment of combat
troops, he did increase the number of military advisers. And
many more would follow later.[39] David Halberstam has argued
persuasively that the Taylor-Rostow Report was critically
decisive. Because Kennedy, in doing less than the recommendations
called for, fell under the false illusion that he was exercising
moderation and caution. While in reality, he was leading the
country ever deeper into the Vietnam mess.[40] At the end of 1961
the total number of military personnel in South Vietnam stood
at 1364, but rose to 9865 at the close of 1962, and was at
almost 16,000 in November of 1963.[41] This would have ominous
repercussions for future planning, since any decision on with-
drawal would now be much more difficult to make. So the Taylor-
Rostow recommendations, which were presented at a time in 1961
when the Vietnam conflict was still at a relatively low level
of intensity, moved American policy away from counterinsurgency
tactics and directed it instead toward more conventional
large-scale warfare.[42]

The question must inevitably be asked why a brilliant young
President, surrounded by supposedly the best and the brightest,
could permit such a thing to happen. One reason often mentioned
is that the issue of Vietnam was still a rather low-level crisis
during the early Kennedy Administration. Certainly at the time
it seemed considerably less pressing than say Cuba, or Berlin, or
even Latin America.[43] In another variation of this argument
there are some observers who claim that Kennedy was embarrassed
and enraged over his rough treatment by Nikita Khrushchev in
Vienna during the late spring of 1961. This, linked with the
fiasco in Cuba, could impel a fledgling world leader to demonstrate in no uncertain terms, through firmness and resolve in
Vietnam, that the United States was not going to knuckle under
to Soviet pressures.[44] And finally, there was the spurious
notion, sustained by American officials in Saigon, that the
strategy of supporting Diem and supplying military advisers
was succeeding.[45]

Whatever illusions Kennedy and his advisers may have enter-
tained about the success of Diem's regime were rudely shattered
in May of 1963 when the South Vietnamese president prohibited
the Buddhists from displaying their flags on the 2587th birthday
of Buddha. To make matters worse, some of Diem's soldiers
fired at a crowd of Buddhists in the city of Hue, and it was at
this point that the situation came apart at the seams. Vietnam
now became a matter requiring the most urgent attention. In
essence, what occurred was the new generation of Vietnamese
nationalists--originating mainly from the middle and lower
classes, who spoke the native language and not French, and who
were Buddhist instead of Catholic--revolting, in all their

xenophobic and hysterical fervor, against the traditional society and classes of Vietnam. The bloody conclusion of the whole affair came when the South Vietnamese army staged a coup, and executed Diem and his brother Nhu.[46] The Pentagon Papers disclose that Kennedy was informed of, and approved, the plans for the coup. Although the American government did not originate the coup, neither did American forces take any action to prevent the assassinations of Diem and Nhu.[47] Then, just three weeks later, Kennedy was dead also, and still another American President inherited the problem.

There will probably always be a debate as to whether or not Kennedy would have reversed American policy toward Vietnam if only he had had a little more time. This is indeed a tantilizing question for any historian, ranking alongside such eternal imponderables of history as whether Lincoln could have spared the nation the agonies of Reconstruction had he not been assassinated, or what the history of the world would have been like had Adolf Hitler died from his wounds in the First World War. Certainly the Kennedy case is no clearer or easier to come to grips with than the other two examples mentioned. The noted journalist, Tom Wicker, is convinced that Kennedy would have changed the country's course in Vietnam. He feels that Kennedy "had consistently labelled the war as one that had to be won or lost by the South Vietnamese--with American help to be sure, but not with Americans doing the fighting."[48] Other observers are not so certain. David Halberstam points out that Kennedy knew full-well the dangers of a deep American involvement, yet he significantly increased that involvement, escalated the number of Americans there greatly, and escalated "the rhetoric and the rationale for being there."[49] Similarly, Chester Cooper, a respected authority on the origins and progress of the war, flatly states that right up until the day of Kennedy's death there was no perceptible evidence that he was prepared to do anything differently in Vietnam.[50] And finally, the Pentagon Papers conclude that President Kennedy had left for Lyndon Johnson a Vietnamese legacy of crisis, instability, and deterioration "at least as alarming to policy makers as the situation he had inherited from the Eisenhower Administration."[51]

To summarize, then, it certainly was not an exaggeration when the noted columnists Rowland Evans and Robert Novak, writing in a 1966 book of theirs, observed: "Lyndon Johnson inherited Vietnam from irrevocable decisions made by his predecessors."[52] And it will be with that President, Lyndon B. Johnson, his decisions on Vietnam, his handling of the war, and the reasons and rationale behind his actions, that the remainder of this study will be devoted. It will be an account of what Johnson did with his inheritance, and why.

CHAPTER ONE

FOOTNOTES

[1] Quoted in Chester L. Cooper, The Lost Crusade: America in Vietnam (New York, 1970), p. 248.

[2] Arthur M. Schlesinger, Jr., The Bitter Heritage: Vietnam and American Democracy, 1941-1966 (Boston, 1966), p. 22.

[3] Cooper, Lost Crusade, p. 18.

[4] Schlesinger, Bitter Heritage, p. 22.

[5] Ibid., pp. 22-23.

[6] Schlesinger, Bitter Heritage, p. 23; Cooper, Lost Crusade, p. 27.

[7] Schlesinger, Ibid., p. 24; Cooper, Ibid., p. 41.

[8] Schlesinger, Ibid: Cooper, Ibid., p. 40.

[9] New York Times, The Pentagon Papers (New York, 1971), p. 8.

[10] Ibid., p. 5; Schlesinger, Bitter Heritage, p. 24.

[11] Pentagon Papers, p. 5.

[12] Ibid., pp. 9-10; Cooper, Lost Crusade, pp. 62-73; Schlesinger, Bitter Heritage, p. 24.

[13] Schlesinger, Ibid., p. 25.

[14] Ibid., pp. 25-26; Cooper, Lost Crusade, pp. 72-73.

[15] Schlesinger, Ibid., p. 26.

[16] Ibid., p. 28.

[17] Pentagon Papers, p. 5.

[18] Schlesinger, Bitter Heritage, p. 28.

17

[19] Ibid., p. 29; Cooper, Lost Crusade, pp. 112-114.

[20] Pentagon Papers, p. 1.

[21] Ibid.

[22] Schlesinger, Bitter Heritage, p. 29.

[23] Cooper, Lost Crusade, p. 135.

[24] Pentagon Papers, pp. 21-22.

[25] Schlesinger, Bitter Heritage, p. 33.

[26] Pentagon Papers, p. 22.

[27] Schlesinger, Bitter Heritage, p. 33.

[28] Ibid.

[29] Pentagon Papers, p. 70

[30] Schlesinger, Bitter Heritage, p. 34.

[31] Ibid., pp. 34-35.

[32] Cooper, Lost Crusade, p. 152.

[33] Schlesinger, Bitter Heritage, pp. 36-37.

[34] David Halberstam, The Best and the Brightest (New York, 1972), p. 41.

[35] Townsend Hoopes, The Limits of Intervention: An Inside Account of How the Johnson Policy of Escalation in Vietnam Was Reversed (New York, 1969), p. 13.

[36] Pentagon Papers, p. 4.

[37] Schlesinger, Bitter Heritage, p. 37.

[38] Ibid., p. 39.

[39] Ibid.

[40] Halberstam, Best and Brightest, p. 177.

[41] Schlesinger, Bitter Heritage, p. 39.

[42]Halberstam, *Best and Brightest*, p. 177; Hoopes, *Limits of Intervention*, p. 23.

[43]Schlesinger, *Bitter Heritage*, p. 40.

[44]Cooper, *Lost Crusade*, p. 8.

[45]Schlesinger, *Bitter Heritage*, p. 40.

[46]*Ibid.*, pp. 43–44.

[47]*Pentagon Papers*, pp. 158–159.

[48]Tom Wicker, *JFK and LBJ: The Influence of Personality Upon Politics* (New York, 1968), p. 191.

[49]Halberstam, *Best and Brightest*, p. 299.

[50]Cooper, *Lost Crusade*, p. 418.

[51]*Pentagon Papers*, p. 113.

[52]Rowland Evans and Robert Novak, *Lyndon B. Johnson: The Exercise of Power* (New York, 1966), p. 530. On this same point see also William Appleman Williams, "Ol Lyndon," *New York Review of Books*, XVII (December 16, 1971), 5–6.

CHAPTER II

LYNDON JOHNSON AND THE VIETNAM WAR

When he ascended to the Presidency on that tragic November day in 1963, Lyndon Johnson inherited a limited war in Vietnam with less than twenty thousand American fighting men committed there. Yet, before his years as President were completed, that limited conflict had been escalated into a mammoth and terribly costly war, with an eventual commitment of over one half millio American men. In the end, this drastic enlargement of the war effort would bitterly divide the nation, and would cost Lyndon Johnson both his popularity and his Presidency. But that was how it ended; the beginning had been quite different.

"There is no word less than superb to describe the performance of Lyndon Baines Johnson as he became President of the United States."[1] This was the assessment of the respected political analyst, Theodore H. White. And White certainly was far from being alone in professing such opinions. Johnson had assumed his high office under tragic and trying circumstances, and he had performed beautifully. He had handled the immense powers and duties of that position with confidence, assurance, and skill. Nor did this performance go unappreciated, as nearl the whole country appreciated and applauded his sincere efforts By the spring of 1964 Johnson was reaping a bountiful harvest of public approval and acclaim. The influential news media was fascinated by him, and intellectuals were thrilled, seeing in Johnson the visage of another Franklin Roosevelt. This great outpouring of popular goodwill and support for the new Chief Executive was clearly reflected in the various opinion polls. In early April of 1964 the Gallup Poll reported that a whopping 77 percent of the American people reacted favorably to the President, and a mere 6 percent viewed him with negative feelings. In the great swell of sympathy following John Kennedy's assassination, the American public was bestowing upon their new leader the generous degree of "consensus" that he so relished, and there was an almost universal conviction that Kennedy had chosen well when he designated Lyndon Johnson to be his Vice-President. There was a relaxed and near euphoric feeling prevalent that the nation was indeed fortunate in having its affairs in such strong and capable hands. Throughout 1964 his position in the polls remained extraordinarily high, with 70 to 80 percent of the populace commonly giving high marks to the President for the way he was handling his job.[2]

Perhaps there is no better example of the tremendous extent of Lyndon Johnson's early popularity than his amazing performance in the election of 1964. Running against conservative candidate Barry Goldwater, LBJ won a resounding victory, amassing in the process more than 60 percent of the vote. However, in retrospect, it was in this same campaign that a frightening portent of things to come first surfaced, an early and crucial element of what would later be described as Johnson's "credibility gap" in regard to the war in Vietnam. For it was in that electoral contest that Johnson, during a speech in Stonewall, Texas, told his audience that he did not intend to widen or escalate the conflict and send "American boys to fighting a war that I think ought to be fought by boys of Asia to help protect their own land. And for that reason, I haven't chosen to enlarge the war."[3] The same theme was developed by the President in Akron, Ohio: "Sometimes our folks get a little impatient. Sometimes they rattle their rockets some, and they bluff about their bombs. But we are not about to send American boys nine or ten thousand miles away from home to do what Asian boys ought to be doing for themselves."[4]

The unmistakable fact is, however, that during the very same time Johnson was expressing these thoughts, and posing as an advocate of peace against the hawkish Goldwater, he was also planning for full-scale air attacks against North Vietnam. In that fateful late fall period of 1964 Lyndon Johnson knew that he was not going to deliver on his promises. The President later informed Charles Roberts, a respected reporter for Newsweek, that he reached his decision to bomb North Vietnam in October of 1964. He told a similar story to the columnist Tom Wicker.[5] The Pentagon Papers reveal that the Johnson Administration may have reached its consensus on bombing as early as September.[6] Certainly by December, just one month after the election, the differences within the Administration between hawks and doves were ending, and the doves were becoming hawks; or as one White House wit put it, they were becoming "dawks," which was an ex-dove who now assumed a more hawkish stance.[7] During the debate, Johnson had attempted to straddle the issue publicly, once saying: "I'm not going north with Curtis LeMay, and I'm not going south with Wayne Morse."[8] But it soon became apparent that LBJ was indeed going north, and at full tilt.

Johnson accomplished this by making it all seem to be just a logical step-by-step sequence of almost unavoidable measures. He and his advisers had prepared carefully; every contingency was noted, and every move was carefully calibrated to respond to the actual or the anticipated actions of the enemy. It was all part of a master plan, and much of that plan had been drawn up well before election day.[9] The Pentagon study shows that the Johnson Administration had begun planning to wage open war as early as the spring of 1964; this was fully a year before the

extent of the involvement became known publicly.[10] Beginning
as early as February or March, 1964, the United States had been
directing covert military attacks against North Vietnam, all
the while devising a plan to obtain a Congressional resolution
that could serve instead of an overt declaration of war.[11] In
July of that year, in retaliation for a North Vietnamese torpedo-
boat attack on American warships, Johnson approved a one-shot
air strike aimed at some torpedo-boat pens and certain other
targets in North Vietnam.[12]

Then on August 2, 1964, there occurred a bizarre incident
in which North Vietnamese torpedo-boats attacked an American
destroyer, the U.S.S. Maddox, in the Gulf of Tonkin. The
initial American response was a protest to Hanoi, and a warning
that there would be reprisals if it should happen again.[13]
Many in Washington were surprised and amazed at the sheer auda-
city and bravado of the North Vietnamese. Appearing at first
like rather foolhardy derring-do by Hanoi, additional details
made it seem more a local act of retaliation for an earlier
South Vietnamese navy raid, rather than a grave and well-
conceived decision by the government of North Vietnam.[14] Then,
inexplicably, on August 4 the North Vietnamese responded with
yet a second attack in the gulf, this time against the Maddox
and the C. Turner Joy. To the President and most of his advisers this second attack was intolerable, taking the form of a
direct insult and affront that had to be answered, and so the
Administration pulled out its previously prepared resolution
for the Congress.[15] In the years since the Tonkin Gulf affair
there has been much scepticism as to whether or not any second
attack ever occurred. The Pentagon Papers make it clear that
it was the physical presence of the American destroyers there
in the area which supplied the main ingredient for the Tonkin
clash.[16] Lending credence to the case of the doubters was the
situation whereby Hanoi owned up to the attack of August 2, but
stated categorically that the allegations of a second attack
were pure fabrications. Also noteworthy is the fact that the
North Vietnamese decorated the P T boat crews participating in
the first encounter; but no laurels were given out for any
second attack.[17]

Whether any second attack did occur or not, the President
went before the nation in a televised message late on the night
of August 4. He informed the public of another unprovoked
attack on the Maddox and the C. Turner Joy by the North
Vietnamese, and of reprisal air raids by the United States.[18]
Just three days later, on August 7, Congress passed the Tonkin
Gulf Resolution, a critical document which gave the Chief Executive sweeping powers for resisting further aggression in
Vietnam. With such a resolution now in hand, Johnson told
Secretary McNamara to be on the alert for another incident which
could justify an escalation of the war.[19] Such an incident did

occur in October of 1964, when Viet Cong guerrillas hit an American air base at Bien Hoa, located only fifteen miles from Saigon. Four Americans were killed, seventy-six were wounded, and six B-57 bombers were destroyed. Then, at Pleiku in February, 1965, a bloody Viet Cong assault killed seven American soldiers and wounded another 109. This was almost exactly the kind of event Johnson had been waiting for, and it furnished him with an excuse for systematic air strikes against North Vietnam.[20] On February 8, 1965, the President issued orders for new reprisal raids against the North Vietnamese. And on February 13, he gave the order for a program of intensive bombing in the North, an operation code-named "Rolling Thunder."[21]

All this was arranged and approved by a man who, just a few short months before, had pledged not to intensify the war. If Lyndon Johnson had not lied, then it was one of the most rapid and miraculous policy conversions in recent American history. Theodore White has remarked that when a President makes a promise not to send American boys to perish in Asian wars, it is incumbent upon that President to "explain why history forces him to break that promise...." But, as White points out, Lyndon Johnson just never saw it that way.[22] For instance, in a news conference some years later when the Vietnam War was at its highest level of intensity, Johnson was confronted with that 1964 compaign promise, and was asked what had changed his policy. The President replied that there had been no change of policy, and then declared: "We always have said--and we repeat now--that we do not want American boys to do the fighting that South Vietnamese boys ought to do or that Asian boys ought to do. We are asking them all to do all they can."[23] Thus, the President seemed to be implying that he had never pledged not to send American boys to fight in Asia, but rather, he had only promised not to have them there fighting alone.

* * * * *

Johnson's old and deeply-ingrained militarism now gained the highest priority in his Administration. |The years from 1964 through 1968 would be filled with one military escalation after another.| The President and his advisers would become obsessed with the notion that a military victory could be won in Vietnam. The result was that millions of his followers became disillusioned when he began neglecting his ambitious domestic plans, something called The Great Society, in order to concentrate on a war against Communist troops which was being acted out on a remote jungle stage some eight or nine thousand miles away from the United States.[24]

Tuesday of each week was an important day for the Johnson Administration. Because Tuesday was the day on which the

President and his closest advisers would invariably meet for
lunch and discussion. This was the so-called "Tuesday Cabinet."
Its agenda was also invariably the same, that is, deliberations
centering on the war in Vietnam and all the tangential issues
which that thorny topic led to. At first, the Chairman of the
Joint Chiefs of Staff, General Earle Wheeler, attended on an
ad hoc arrangement. But after early 1966 his presence became
much more frequent, as there was now a growing consensus that
the solution in Vietnam would come through military means, not
diplomatic. In line with this conviction, the Director of the
Central Intelligence Agency, Richard Helms, also began to appear at the meetings.[25] Thus, to the men of the Tuesday Cabinet,
the war had begun to take new directions early in 1966. It now
seemed that a military solution was more practicable than a
political or diplomatic arrangement, and the planning now reflected this new set of assumptions. And, of course, the tone
of these plans was set by, and reflected the mood and temper
of, the President and his chief consultants.[26]

In relation to Johnson's mood and temper, the President
stated that all he desired was to allow the South Vietnamese
people freedom of choice. In a statement on Vietnam in 1965,
LBJ had proclaimed that the policy of the United States was
"to furnish assistance to support South Viet-Nam for as long
as is required to bring Communist aggression and terrorism under
control." He went on to say that American military actions
would be used only to serve that purpose--"at the lowest possible
cost in human life to our allies, to our own men, and to our
adversaries, too."[27] The whole problem was, however, that his
conditions for a political settlement left very little leeway
for any real bargaining. More and more a clear military victory
for the United States became implicit in any satisfactory
settlement.[28] Townsend Hoopes, former Deputy Assistant Secretary
of Defense for International Affairs, and Under Secretary of
the Air Force, has written that nearly everything which was
tragic and wrong about Johnson's war policy "flowed from the
assumption that we could, within the bounds of recognizably
'limited war,' win a military victory in Vietnam," or along the
same lines, to force the North Vietnamese and Viet Cong to accept American terms through military power.[29] Time and again
Johnson claimed that he was only trying to fulfill the nation's
solemn commitment to freedom in South Vietnam; but his conduct
of the war revealed a President who was prepared to expend
armies, dollars, and men without limit.[30]

On April 1, 1965, President Johnson reached the decision
to deploy American ground troops for combat purposes in South
Vietnam. The Administration was aware that its carefully
planned bombing of North Vietnam, which had only recently been
initiated, would just not be sufficient. After arriving at his
troop decision, the President ordered that the plan be kept

secret. Several months later, the Under Secretary of State, George Ball, presented Johnson with a memorandum which proposed a compromise solution for South Vietnam. But the President and most of his advisers were in no mood for compromise; LBJ was much more attentive to General William Westmoreland's recommendation for embarking upon a large-scale ground war. So on June 26, General Westmoreland was granted the authority to send United States forces into battle when he deemed it necessary.[31] As the Pentagon Papers note, this grant of authority "was about as close to a free hand in managing the forces as General Westmoreland was likely to get."[32]

With the fateful decision once made, the rapid expansion of American forces during 1965 and 1966 was nothing short of stupendous. It was during this initial build-up that a crucial and tragic miscalculation took place. The Johnson Administration was operating under the delusion that continual American reinforcement would create the necessary margin of military superiority. This was far from being the case, however. Because the enemy forces matched every escalation and increase by the United States, which served only to edge the conflict upward to a higher and bloodier stalemate. It became obvious that the North Vietnamese and Viet Cong could match every step of intensification right up to the point of nuclear war, an alternative which was unthinkable even for Lyndon Johnson.[33] As the Pentagon study observes, the ability of the enemy forces "to build up their effort was consistently underrated."[34]

The outcome of this unanticipated build-up capacity by the enemy was that General Westmoreland's troop requests took on a concomitant increase. His requests rose from a total of 175,000 men in June, 1965, up to 275,000 for July, then jumped from 443,000 in December all the way up to 542,000 the following June.[35] These gigantic demands for more men by Westmoreland won quick approval by the President; in a press conference of February, 1966, Johnson had made very clear his position on the General's appeals for more troops when he promised: "As he makes his requests, they will be considered and they will be met."[36] Along with the massive troop increases, the Johnson Administration was also continually expanding the air war during 1965 and 1966.[37] The escalation of the war in the air was likewise predicated on what the Pentagon Papers describes as a "colossal misjudgement", a serious overestimation concerning the effect of the bombing on Hanoi's morale and capabilities.[38]

Johnson, far from being depressed about the constant need for escalation, seemed to be immensely proud of the great military effort. On one occasion, when talking with the historian Henry Graff, the President expressed a great deal of pride about the way the United States had then moved between 150,000 and

200,000 men into Vietnam, all with what he described as "the greatest efficiency in the history of the world". Johnson talked on and on about the military hospitals which had been constructed and the new housing which was going up there. LBJ, Graff recalls, quoted with pleasure and approval General Westmoreland's statement describing the army as "the most mobile under any flag, the best equipped, and the one with the most firepower per man." The President was equally pleased with the statistics in relation to casualties. He told Graff: "We have the lowest ratio of wounded to dead we've ever had—three to one."[39] If anything, Johnson placed progressively greater reliance upon the military as the months passed. By the spring of 1968 the President was continuing to lean heavily on the advice of his generals and their views on the war. There was even talk that General Westmoreland would soon ask for an additional 200,000 men for combat.[40]

* * * * *

General Westmoreland's request for 200,000 more fighting men set off a sharp and prolonged policy debate in the Johnson Administration during the spring of 1967. In fact, the story of the Johnson Presidency from late 1966 onward is that of an Administration at odds with itself, due to the rising pressures of an ever-lengthening war and the changing views of some key senior policymakers.[41] One of the most significant and disturbing policy turnabouts for the President was that of Defense Secretary Robert S. McNamara. The Pentagon study reveals that McNamara had tried as early as October of 1966 to persuade Johnson to institute a cutback in the bombing of North Vietnam in order to pursue a political settlement—a full seventeen months before any such action was taken by the Chief Executive. This change of heart by the Secretary of Defense, who had formerly been a strong proponent of the bombing strategy and a firm believer in the efficacy of American intervention, ushered in a deep policy breach in the Johnson Administration.[42]

The Pentagon Papers describe three principal divisions within the Administration. First, there was the group known as the "disillusioned doves". This was the McNamara faction, seeking to limit and reduce the war. Then there was the military clique representing the Joint Chiefs of Staff and General Westmoreland, agitating and pressing for an even wider war. And finally, there was the President and certain civilian officials, at both the White House and the State Department, who were attempting to take a middle position.[43]

The real climax for the "disillusioned doves" came on May 19, 1967 when Secretary McNamara presented Johnson with a frank memorandum. In that memorandum, McNamara lined up all the arguments against the proposed strategy of widening the war, and marshaled the evidence in favor of a curtailment of the air war. This May 19 paper of McNamara's urged a cutback of all bombing to the 20th Parallel, and even more pointedly, suggested that General Westmoreland's request be pared down to only 30,000 more troops, instead of the original figure of 200,000. Going a step further, the Secretary argued that the Johnson Administration should cease its attempts at guaranteeing a non-Communist South Vietnam; rather, he recommended that the President be receptive to the possibility of a coalition government for Saigon, which would include representation of the Viet Cong elements.[44] However, LBJ was considerably less than enthusiastic about McNamara's proposals. And during July and August the President embraced a course of action regarding the air war which was far removed from the pleas for de-escalation which Secretary McNamara had made. On November 28, 1967, Johnson nominated McNamara to be president of the World Bank, replacing him as Secretary of Defense.[45]

What McNamara and the "disillusioned doves" could not accomplish, the enemy's Tet offensive, in February of 1968, did. This big offensive during Tet, the Lunar New Year, commenced on January 31 when an attack was mounted against the United States Embassy in Saigon. The embassy compound was held by the enemy guerrilla forces for an entire day. Then the attacks diffused over a wide area, hitting nearly all the cities and principal towns of South Vietnam. Even Hue, the ancient capital of central Vietnam, suffered capture, and it was not liberated until the very final stages of the offensive, on February 24.[46] These attacks by the enemy, striking almost at will along the entire length and breadth of South Vietnam, sent deep shock waves reverberating through official circles in Washington.

The offensive had taken the White House and the Joint Chiefs by surprise, and they were genuinely shocked and amazed at the strength and prolonged intensity of the attacks. For the President, the jolt and chagrin were especially severe. During much of 1967 Johnson had discounted and disregarded some of the more negative analyses on American strategy given him by the Central Intelligence Agency and other agencies. Rather, LBJ had eagerly grasped the more optimistic reports presented him by General Westmoreland.[47] But now, in the wake of Tet, the illusions were shattered. The Pentagon Papers point out that the disillusionment and turmoil of the Tet offensives galvanized the Joint Chiefs of Staff and General Westmoreland into action. They began putting heavy pressure on the President to move in the direction of national mobilization in a desperate effort to salvage a victory in Vietnam. It was these military proposals which set off the final and acrimonious policy debate within the Administration, a debate which would eventually see the military's desires spurned.[48]

Clark M. Clifford was the man chosen to succeed Robert
McNamara as Secretary of Defense. Clifford was an old and
trusted adviser of the President's, and he would play a key role
in the reversal of the Johnson war policies. On February 28,
Generals Wheeler and Westmoreland submitted a report to the
President stating the military's position. It was at this
juncture that LBJ requested that Clifford summon together a
group of advisers, with the intention of completely reviewing
the policy of the United States in Vietnam.[49]

By March of 1968, the alternatives had become vividly under-
standable. It was now clear that the costs of a military victory
had risen immeasurably, with the distinct possibility that they
would continue to grow in the future. Even more disturbing,
there were now powerful indications that large percentages of
the American public believed the price of the war had reached
too high a level, and would be strongly opposed to any further
large increments in that cost.[50] Johnson's popularity in the
country had certainly plummeted drastically. The President fell
precipitously from a 70 percent approval for his policies and
performance in 1965 all the way down to a 39 percent reading in
August of 1967. During the spring of 1968 Senator Eugene J.
McCarthy of Minnesota contested with Johnson for the party's
nomination, and gained a near-victory over the President in the
New Hampshire primary in March. By September, LBJ's popularity
would skid to an all-time low when only 35 percent of the American
people, as polled by Gallup, believed the President was doing an
acceptable job.[51]

With the relentless tide of events pressing in upon him,
the President made one last tilt at the old windmill of victory
in Vietnam. Speaking before a midwestern audience on March 17,
Johnson proclaimed: "Your President has come here to ask you
people, and all the other people of this nation, to join us in
a total national effort to win the war....Make no mistake about
it...we are going to win"[52] But the handwriting was now on the
wall. In a surprise move on March 22, Johnson recalled General
Westmoreland and made public his intention of appointing the
General to be Chief of Staff of the Army. This transfer of
Westmoreland was the prime indicator that the President had
finally decided against another large escalation of the ground
war.[53] Following this, on March 26, Johnson met with his senior
advisers in the Cabinet Room. In discussions which Theodore White
says "must have been shattering for the President", Johnson
discovered that very few hawks were left. The consensus of
opinion emerging out of this meeting was that the nation had
become mired down in the quicksand of a war against Asian guerrillas, a war that could now only be won by major escalation
and the risk of a disastrous war with China. It was generally
agreed that the proper course of action for the future would be
to halt the bombings and begin plans for a negotiated

settlement.[54] And in the final act of the tragic Johnson drama, the President announced to the nation on the evening of March 31 the proposed bombing halt, and in another surprise move, his own decision not to be a candidate for the Presidency again. So in this final, ironic twist of fate, Lyndon Johnson's own political career became a casualty of the war he had done so much to escalate and widen.

* * * * *

This, in short, is what one American President did with an inherited war. Though not a war of his own making, his policies and decisions with regard to that conflict would bring bitterness and tragedy to his country and to his career. The foregoing have been the depressing series of happenings and events which brought a President, and nearly a nation, to ruin. This has been a brief recounting of <u>what</u> took place. But an even more fascinating aspect of the story is <u>why</u> all this occurred, and it is to such an investigation that we now turn.

CHAPTER TWO

FOOTNOTES

[1]Theodore H. White, The Making of the President 1964 (New York, 1965), p. 31.

[2]Richard Harwood and Haynes Johnson, Lyndon (New York, 1973), pp. 51; 64.

[3]Quoted in Eric F. Goldman, The Tragedy of Lyndon Johnson (New York, 1969), p. 235.

[4]Quoted in Philip Geyelin, Lyndon B. Johnson and the World (New York, 1966), p. 197.

[5]Tom Wicker, JFK and LBJ: The Influence of Personality Upon Politics (New York, 1968), p. 232.

[6]New York Times, The Pentagon Papers (New York, 1971), p. 307.

[7]Charles Roberts, LBJ's Inner Circle (New York, 1965), p. 23.

[8]Quoted in Ibid.

[9]Geyelin, Johnson and the World, p. 214.

[10]Pentagon Papers, p. xi.

[11]Ibid., p. 234.

[12]Geyelin, Johnson and the World, p. 113.

[13]Ibid., p. 190.

[14]Chester L. Cooper, The Lost Crusade: America in Vietnam (New York, 1970), p. 239.

[15]Geyelin, Johnson and the World, pp. 190-191; Pentagon Papers, p. 234.

[16]Pentagon Papers, p. 240.

[17] Cooper, Lost Crusade, p. 241.

[18] Alfred Steinberg, Sam Johnson's Boy: A Close-Up of the President From Texas (New York, 1968), p. 765.

[19] Ibid., p. 768.

[20] Ibid., pp. 768-769; Geyelin, Johnson and the World, p. 11.

[21] Pentagon Papers, p. 310.

[22] Theodore H. White, The Making of the President 1968 (New York, 1969), p. 116.

[23] U. S., National Archives and Records Service, Public Papers of the Presidents of the United States: Lyndon B. Johnson, VIII, Doc. 460, November 1, 1967, 971.

[24] Steinberg, Sam Johnson's Boy, p. 696.

[25] Henry F. Graff, The Tuesday Cabinet: Deliberation and Decision on Peace and War under Lyndon B. Johnson (Englewood Cliffs, 1970), pp. 3-4.

[26] Ibid., p. 68.

[27] Public Papers, III, Doc. 130, March 25, 1965, 319.

[28] Townsend Hoopes, The Limits of Intervention: An Inside Account of How the Johnson Policy of Escalation in Vietnam Was Reversed (New York, 1969), p. 58.

[29] Ibid., p. 186.

[30] Ibid., p. 58.

[31] Pentagon Papers, pp. 382-414.

[32] Ibid., p. 414.

[33] Arthur M. Schlesinger, Jr., The Bitter Heritage: Vietnam and American Democracy, 1941-1966 (Boston, 1966), p. 58.

[34] Pentagon Papers, p. 459.

[35] Ibid.

[36] Public Papers, V, Doc. 88, February 26, 1966, 226.

[37] Pentagon Papers, p. 459.

[38] Ibid.

[39] Graff, _Tuesday Cabinet_, pp. 97-98.

[40] Ibid., p. 153.

[41] _Pentagon Papers_, pp. 511; 527.

[42] Ibid., p. 510.

[43] Ibid., p. 511.

[44] Ibid., pp. 535; 510.

[45] Ibid., pp. 539-540; 510.

[46] Ibid., p. 592.

[47] Ibid.

[48] Ibid., p. 589.

[49] Ibid.

[50] Ibid., p. 611.

[51] Harwood and Johnson, _Lyndon_, pp. 123; 138.

[52] Quoted in Hoopes, _Limits of Intervention_, p. 206.

[53] _Pentagon Papers_, p. 609.

[54] White, _Making of the President 1968_, p. 130.

CHAPTER III

SOME EXPLANATIONS FOR ESCALATION

In the last chapter there was recounted some of the important decisions made during the Johnson Presidency which significantly enlarged and widened the war which that President had inherited. Yet to observe merely the events is not enough; also necessary is a probing into the underlying reasons and rationale for those actions. No world leader in history has stood alone, shaping and channeling events to suit his personal whim and caprice. Rather, every leader is to some extent a prisoner of the past, being subtly influenced by the men and events which have preceded him, being at least occasionally affected by great and impersonal forces already set in motion. This was certainly the case with Lyndon Baines Johnson. Although his deeds speak loudly, there were, nevertheless, certain compelling reasons which go far to explain his behavior.

* * * * *

For one thing, there were the myriad of pressures which descend upon any new President, especially one who comes to the Oval Office through the agency of death or assassination. The world situation confronted by Lyndon Johnson when he assumed the Presidency was one tossed and buffeted by serious national, regional, religious, and ideological differences. It was a concatenation of problems which would not lend themselves to great and sweeping solutions, or to well-conceived and brilliant diplomatic master strokes. Neither was it a world which would be willing to grovel before American military power.[1]

Combined with this difficult and tense world situation, was the fact that he was after all a new President. He was a man who had practiced the art of politics for nearly a generation, yet was in many respects virtually an unknown quantity in the minds of many of his countrymen. In addition, among those who did know him, he was not universally understood or even trusted in all cases. He succeeded John Kennedy late in the third year of his term, which meant that in a mere six months or so the Democratic Party would pass judgment upon him by deciding whether or not to nominate him for 1964. And if he did receive the nomination, this meant that in less than a year the entire nation would be passing judgment upon his leadership.[2]

So in those early days of his Presidency, Johnson was under tremendous strain. On the one hand, he faced a fierce and unpredictable world which he was still largely unfamiliar with; and on the other, he was moved by an intense desire, perhaps part of the famous Johnson ego, to prove to everyone that he could handle the nation's foreign affairs.[3] He realized that, ready or not, great and immense duties had been thrust upon him. A shocked and stunned nation had to be reassured that their government was still functioning the same, that it was not paralyzed. Johnson knew that it was imperative for him to grasp the reins of power, that there could be no doubts or hesitation, that it had to be done without delay. The new Chief Executive was also keenly aware that the entire world was watching the crisis in the United States closely. The national security demanded that there be no signs of weakness or indecision, since these could have dark and dangerous international repercussions-- in Berlin, in Latin America, and in Southeast Asia. The entire world, whether friendly or hostile, had to be shown that the policies of the United States would be continued by this new and untested leader. There could be no equivocating, there could be nothing which would seem to other countries that the government of the United States was faltering.[4] In his memoirs, Johnson vividly recalled all those pressures: "I had to convince everyone everywhere that the country would go forward, that the business of the United States would proceed. I knew that not only the nation but the whole world would be anxiously following every move I made--watching, judging, weighing, balancing."[5]

Thus, it was not an easy time for a new President inheriting his office during the last days of 1963. No matter which way he turned, there were obligations and commitments which could not be ducked.[6] The American people seemed more concerned about international affairs than they did about those of a domestic nature. They had expressed themselves as being in favor of alliances, of which there were now more than forty, all approved and ratified by their representatives in the Senate. A significant number of those alliances were with countries located in the Pacific area. There had been security pacts and mutual defense treaties signed with Australia, New Zealand, and the Philippines during 1951, with the Republic of Korea and the Republic of China in 1953 and 1954, and with many countries in the Southeast Asia Treaty Organization of 1954. Following this, the United States had signed a treaty with Japan in 1960. And several polls taken after the conflict in Korea had indicated majorities favoring aid to the other nations in Asia who might be faced with Communist aggression. Taken as a whole then, it would seem to Lyndon Johnson in 1963 that there was a clear indication of what the country expected of him in regard to Southeast Asia.[7]

During the Kennedy years, the American people had been nar-
rowly divided on many issues. Yet, there was one bedrock issue
which a President had to be aware of, one certainty in American
politics which he could not neglect--that any Chief Executive
who did not follow a strong line against the "Communists" would
be extremely vulnerable. Such a President would be susceptible
to attack by both political opponents at home and by designing
foreign adversaries. And these adversaries at home and abroad
would be especially diligent in scrutinizing a fledgling leader.
All his politics, attitudes, and responses would be examined
under a magnifying glass, and any weakness detected would be
ominously noted. And above all else, Lyndon Johnson realized
that he had to be strong, or at least give the vital appearance
of strength.[8]

Vietnam is a case in point. If he should display weakness
as a President in coping with Vietnam, LBJ was convinced that it
would jeopardize his chances politically. He vividly recalled
how Truman and Dean Acheson had been blamed by the Republicans
in Congress for the loss of China, and how Truman's support in
the Congress and the country had dwindled dangerously. The
crisis had not been caused over domestic affairs, but rather,
over foreign issues. So the last thing this pressed and uncertain President wanted was to be blamed for losing Vietnam,
because such an occurrence could well lead to the loss of the
rest of his program.[9] Johnson fully realized the political
importance of Vietnam when he commented: "If I don't go in now
and they show later I should have gone, then they'll be all over
me in Congress. They won't be talking about my civil rights
bill, or education or beautification. No sir, they'll push
Vietnam up my ass every time. Vietnam. Vietnam. Vietnam.
Right up my ass."[10]

Thus, to a new and uncertain President there seemed to be a
great deal of wisdom and security in adopting the Vietnam policy
of the previous Administration, in emphasizing a "continuity"
theme. Johnson wrote in his memoirs of how on Air Force One,
returning from that tragic trip to Dallas on November 22, 1963,
he vowed he would work to achieve John Kennedy's unfulfilled
goals, including his stand on Vietnam. LBJ declared: "I made
this promise not out of blind loyalty but because I was convinced that the broad lines of his policy, in Southeast Asia and
elsewhere, had been right. They were consistent with the goals
the United States had been trying to accomplish in the world
since 1945."[11] During one of Johnson's first days in the White
House he met with Henry Cabot Lodge, American Ambassador to
South Vietnam, and assured him that he, Lyndon Johnson, was "not
going to be the President who saw Southeast Asia go the way China
went."[12] Just before Kennedy's death, his closest aides attended
a strategy conference on Vietnam in Honolulu. Just four days
after that meeting, Johnson put out a new policy paper on Vietnam

which demonstrated convincingly that there was not going to be any break from President Kennedy's policies.[13] The Pentagon Papers note this "continuity" theme, finding that there was an unbroken chain of decision-making from the last months of the Kennedy Administration into the first months of the Johnson Administration.[14]

* * * * *

The journalist Charles Roberts, in a 1965 book on LBJ's "inner circle", concluded his examination with a most perceptive prediction. Roberts wrote: "The achievement of The Great Society, the maintenance of peace and prosperity--the success or failure of the Johnson Administration--will hinge more on the wisdom and competence of the President's advisers than history may ever acknowledge."[15] Harry Zeiger, in a 1963 book on Johnson assuming the Presidency, put it even more succinctly, perhaps to the point of understatement, when he observed: "The men around any President can have a great effect on him."[16] These comments are of critical importance in regard to Lyndon Johnson. Because President Johnson inherited more than just a perplexing war in Vietnam. He also inherited John Kennedy's chief advisers on foreign policy--men like Rusk, McNamara, Bundy, Rostow, and Taylor.[17]

And Johnson certainly was not adverse to this. It has been pointed out previously how the new President very much wanted to present an appearance of continuity between the two Administrations. President Johnson strongly pleaded with the Kennedy staff to stay. Johnson had a number of excellent reasons for wanting to hold on to these men. For one thing, it was just good taste and good politics to allow the Kennedy group to remain. But even more important, Kennedy's people were extremely knowledgeable, and it would have taken Johnson many months to build up a staff of comparable quality. In addition, the Kennedy people found it hard to say no to the sincere request of a man who had so suddenly been thrust with all the problems and burdens of the Presidency. The Kennedy team would have severely disrupted any display of orderly transition in government had they refused. So the President was very successful in convincing staff Cabinet members, and aides to stay on, and the transition of power was accomplished smoothly and swiftly.[18]

All this meant that there would be a minimum of interruptio with the Kennedy view. This implied further that the Eisenhower and Kennedy commitments to South Vietnam would have to be respected. Even more importantly, it meant that the major architects of the Vietnamese involvement were now going to be Johnson's advisers.[19] And the dominant train of thought among these close advisers was deeply rooted in what might be called the old "Cold War Syndrome." They thought in terms of treaties, alignments, and alliances. They still saw the Communist threat as an essentially monolithic conspiracy emanating from Moscow and Peking, and manifesting its sinister designs through military and paramilitary attacks against the so-called "Free World." Corresponding to this view of the world was the belief that Communist aggression had to be checked wherever it occurred, or the existing world power balance would be irrevocably eroded.[20] Five of President Johnson's most important policy advisers inherited from the Kennedy years held this conception of the world scene.

There was Dean Rusk, Secretary of State. Townsend Hoopes has written that of the close advisers on Vietnam, Dean Rusk "seemed the very embodiment of the embattled Cold Warrior...."[21] To Rusk, the old conflict between the Communists and the free world was as basic and as fundamental as any conflict could be. He once remarked in this regard: "Their proclaimed objectives and our conception of a decent world order just do not and cannot fit together."[22] From the very beginning he had taken a strong position on Vietnam, and he had found Lyndon Johnson to be very attentive to his views. Rusk urged a relentless prosecution of the conflict, and few doubted the preponderant force of his advice in the Presidential conferences.[23] Once when replying to critics, Dean Rusk reduced the Vietnam conflict to its lowest terms when he stated that "one thing really hasn't gotten into their gizzards," and that was that the United States meant what it said about its commitments.[24]

There was Robert S. McNamara, Secretary of Defense. Often during 1964 the fighting in Vietnam was termed "McNamara's War." He was the man who took charge of the war in the early days of the Johnson Administration, a time when Secretary Rusk was keeping more in the background publicly. Although sometimes more reluctant about the course of United States strategy in Vietnam in later years, he nevertheless was the man who kept in close touch with all the various aspects of that conflict. Through brilliant calculations and analyses he would do much to lend a sense of feasibility to the war in the early stages, and thus set the tone for much of the policy which came later.[25]

There was General Maxwell Taylor, consultant to President Johnson and head of the Institute for Defense Analyses. Taylor had been the perfect Kennedy-type general, always articulate and always presentable. His views on the war in Vietnam were consistent and predictable. Taylor time and again firmly insisted that the country should work for a military victory in Vietnam, a policy of unrelenting military pressure. The war, as he saw it, was a plain case of aggression by North Vietnam, and the only sensible solution was to force the enemy to give up the fight in the South.[26]

There was McGeorge Bundy, the special presidential assistant for national security affairs. A former Harvard dean, he did much to lend an air of academic respectability to the war. He sent a memorandum to President Johnson, in February of 1965, which argued in favor of a full-scale bombing campaign against the North. Bundy assured the President that his recommendation, when "measured against the costs of defeat in Vietnam...seems cheap. And even if it fails to turn the tide...the value of the effort seems to us to exceed its costs."[27]

And there was Walt Rostow, head of the Policy Planning Staff. He perceived the war in Vietnam as one more instance of a centrally directed and executed Communist challenge. Rostow was certain that Communist success there would ignite a chain of revolutionary conflagrations in other vulnerable areas throughout the world. To him, it was clear that the Communist challenge in Vietnam had to be met and turned back.[28] John Kennedy had once said of his aide that he was "a fountain of ideas; perhaps one in ten of them is absolutely brilliant. Unfortunately, six or seven are not merely unsound, but dangerously so."[29]

Thus, all five of these key advisers for Lyndon Johnson were in favor of American combat measures in Vietnam.[30] After a series of conversations with Johnson's advisers, Henry Graff got the distinct impression that while these men were not exactly speaking of conquest in the war, they were nevertheless resolved not to accept defeat either. After all, they had played a big role in the building of the Vietnam commitment, and they were well aware that they, too, would be held accountable by history if it were not brought to a satisfactory conclusion. In other words, Johnson had inherited a set of advisers who had a stake in the continuance of a Vietnam involvement.[31] In this light, it can perhaps be argued that military escalation became almost inevitable in 1965 when a new President, uncertain and insecure in the realm of foreign affairs, was teamed up with a group of close advisers who, in the words of one observer, "reinforced his own tendency to think about the external world in the simplistic terms of appeasement versus military resolve."[32]

* * * * *

If Lyndon Johnson gained encouragement for his Vietnam policies from his closest advisers, he was also sustained by the memory of certain men and events in the American past. There were many clear and definite precedents in the country's previous experience, and in the actions of Presidential predecessors, for almost every action undertaken by Johnson in regard to the Vietnam War. This is not to argue that LBJ's actions can be justified or legitimized in the light of what was done in other times, but it does serve to point out that a President carrying out such a policy could gain comfort from the realization that he was well within the bounds of the American tradition. And it is that tradition, in terms of Presidents and military actions, which will now be considered.

There is nothing new about American military interventions in various parts of the world. The American experience is full of previous interventions undertaken without congressional declarations of war; in fact, past Presidents had committed troops on at least 150 different occasions. And some of these operations had been very well publicized. There was nothing secret about President McKinley sending troops to China in 1900 to aid in squelching the Boxer Rebellion. Likewise, President Theodore Roosevelt dispatched soldiers to Panama, Cuba, and the Dominican Republic. And in similar fashion, President Wilson had ordered an American expedition to capture Vera Cruz in 1914.[33]

Neither was there anything novel or unique about Lyndon Johnson promising in the midst of a Presidential campaign not to commit American boys to a foreign war, and then reversing himself following the election. There were other examples of that same phenomenon in the American past. For example, during the last days of the presidential campaign in 1916, while war was raging in Europe, Woodrow Wilson posed as the peace candidate. He criticized the Republicans as "the war party," and solemnly assured his audiences that he was "not expecting this country to get into war." His most successful slogan during that race was "He kept us out of the war." But then, a scant four months later that same man, President Wilson, was standing before the Congress pleading for a declaration of war against Germany.[34] Likewise, during the 1940 campaign, when the rumblings of war were being heard once again in Europe and the Far East, Franklin D. Roosevelt just as solemnly informed a crowd in Boston: "And while I am talking to you mothers and fathers, I give you one more assurance. I have said this before, but I shall say it again and again and again: Your boys are not going to be sent into any foreign wars." Within fourteen months, American boys were waging war in both Europe and Asia.[35]

Likewise, the Johnson technique of waiting for the enemy to provide a pretext for wider war had firm grounding in the American tradition. John F. Kennedy had given expression to that idea when he declared in his Inaugural Address: "Our arms will never be used to strike the first blow in any attack. It is our national tradition."[36] This "national tradition" which Kennedy spoke of was indeed a strong one. Perhaps much of its strength was derived from what might be called the "democratic ideal," the notion that the people inhabiting a democracy are inclined by nature to be peace-loving. Although such people will not precipitate a war, or so the argument runs, they will be quick in their righteous indignation to avenge insults or repel attacks.[37] An American leader, therefore, must convince his fellow countrymen of the deliberate or evil intent of another power before the country is prepared to bear the hardships and sacrifices of war. But if it requires the enemy striking the initial blow to galvanize the patriotism and fighting spirit of the American people, it also leaves that leader open to charges of inventing or contriving the crucial attack.[38] And this has been the case several times during the course of American history; there have been a number of Tonkin Gulf incidents in that national experience.

This custom of having the enemy always strike first runs like a red thread through the entire tapestry of American warfare. It began with the Revolutionary War, when on that historic morning of April 19, 1775, the British approached the patriots assembled on the green at Lexington, and according to American accounts, proceeded to fire at the Minutemen, precipitating the war which would eventually result in American independence. However, once gained, that independence had to be defended. So in 1812 Americans once again fought the British. And once again, Americans were convinced that Great Britain had perpetrated deliberate aggression through such actions as impressing American seamen and hampering American trade. The major incident here was a British ship, the Leopard, firing upon a war vessel of the United States, an affair which has been described as the "Pearl Harbor of the War of 1812."[39]

Moving into the middle period of American history, the situations required for warfare remained the same. In 1846 President James K. Polk had sent an army into a disputed area around the Rio Grande River. Not surprisingly, these troops had been allegedly fired on by Mexican soldiers, and Polk requested from Congress a declaration of war. The President informed the Congress that "American blood has been shed upon American soil," and that war existed due to the actions of Mexico. This was the first time, but not the last, that an American President was accused of going out of his way to bring about an attack in order to excite the citizenry for the necessity of war. Ironically, a congressman from Illinois, named Abraham Lincoln, was one of Polk's severest critics on that count. This was ironic because in 1861 this same Abraham Lincoln, now President, was also charged with sending a military force into contested territory to invite the other side's aggression, and he would become the second Chief Executive to be suspected of contriving a war.[40] In what one author has described as "Abraham Lincoln's Tonkin Gulf," the President had his pretext for what he may have concluded was inevitable civil war, when a cannon on the shore of Charleston Harbor fired the first shot at Fort Sumter. The decision for war, if not any easier, was now made more palatable to the North after soldiers and property of the United States had been the targets of Confederate aggression.[41]

Similarly, Presidents in more recent times have been careful
to shift the onus and blame for war upon another country. For
example, in 1898 McKinley's decision for war with Spain was
facilitated by the blowing up of the <u>Maine</u>. In 1917, when
Woodrow Wilson saw no alternative to American participation in
World War I, the memory of the sinking of the <u>Lusitania</u> lended
credence to his accusation of war-provoking submarine warfare
on the part of Germany. And in 1941, Franklin Roosevelt's anxiety about United States neutrality conveniently ended when
Japan suddenly attacked Pearl Harbor. It was so convenient, in
fact, that Roosevelt became the President perhaps most bitterly
denounced for allegedly maneuvering the nation into war.[42]

Finally, Vietnam was not the first unpopular war in United
States history, nor was Lyndon Johnson the first maligned and
vilified wartime President. Other American wars have been quite
controversial and distasteful to sizeable portions of the
country's populace. For example, the War of 1812 was marked by a
tremendous amount of dissent, and it was that war which originated the word "hawks" and provided the term "Mr. Madison's
War" which would later serve as a precedent for the epithet of
Mr. Johnson's War. That war was an extraordinarily controversial
affair, one that generated a large amount of heated dissent,
especially in the New England area. In a similar manner, the
Mexican War in the years 1846-48 witnessed powerful opposition
in the halls of Congress. As noted before, Congressman Abraham
Lincoln was a vociferous critic of that war, and Lincoln was
joined in his dissent by many concerned citizens, as well as
influential editors and writers. Then just a few years later,
Lincoln himself was confronted with the same kind of criticism
and dissent as the bloody reality of prolonged civil war dis-
couraged many of his fellow citizens. Lincoln's heavy burdens
as a wartime leader were then experienced to some extent by
Presidents Wilson and Roosevelt during the two world wars, but
it was during the Korean War that really widespread dissent
occurred again. Polls indicated that by early 1951 about
half of the American population considered the conflict a mistake, while others felt that Congress should handle the dis-
patching of troops overseas, and many more expressed alarm about
the great increases in the cost of living. Such deep-seated
discontent and unrest had a disastrous effect on President
Truman's popularity. By the end of 1951 a mere 23 percent of
those polled registered approval for the way Truman was performing as President.[43]

And so during all the sound and fury engendered by the war
in Vietnam, President Lyndon Johnson could draw comfort from the
realization that all the insults and mockery which were being
directed at him had also been experienced by some of his
greatest predecessors during their tenure in the White House,
men who had later won vindication and glory in the history

books.[44] Inspired by these reminders, Johnson wrapped about his shoulders the mantle of War Leader, and determined to stand strong in the face of the torrent of abuse, to defend the faith passed down from on high by Lincoln, Wilson, and Roosevelt. These men had suffered the slings and arrows of public disdain, had defied public opinion, and had received their just reward when later generations praised their wisdom and courage, and called them great.[45] LBJ saw himself as the legitimate heir of those enshrined wartime leaders; he received satisfaction from playing the role of an embattled President. Once at a news conference when being pressed hard on the war issue, Johnson called on the memory of those other wartime Chief Executives: "I don't need to remind you of what happened in the Civil War. People were here in the White House begging Lincoln to concede and to work out a deal with the Confederacy.... I think you know what Roosevelt went through, and President Wilson in World War I...."[46] And in his memoirs, LBJ is very frank about his debt to those men of the past. Johnson wrote: "Throughout those years of crucial decisions I was sustained by the memory of my predecessors who had also borne the most painful duty of a President--to lead our country in a time of war."[47]

* * * * *

Lyndon Johnson's actions regarding Vietnam were well within the perimeters of the American experience. They were also very much in line with his own past experience. Johnson was not a scholar; he had no deep grounding in such disciplines as history or philosophy. His learning was gained from a lifetime of public service, years spent as a congressman and senator, as a Vice President, and finally as a President.[48] During that career of some thirty years he had observed and played some role in almost every important action of the United States. There were few other men still alive who had such a vast storehouse of contemporary experience. The important lesson which Johnson gleaned from the span of history he had lived through was that when the country ignored defense or world responsibilities, trouble was the usual outcome. And that trouble was generally worse than it would have been had firm leadership faced up to the problem earlier.[49]

These principles absorbed by Lyndon Johnson were not the result of any abstract speculation, rather, they were the fruits of his own personal experience. While still a young man in Congress he had seen the nation's failure to prepare for the Second World War. This was a failure caused at least in part by the strong isolationist sentiment in Congress.[50] With Hitler on the move during late 1941, Johnson perceived that it was vital for the country to forget about neutrality and begin planning for war.[51] Johnson had been with Roosevelt when he turned away from the New Deal in order to concentrate on fighting a war.

42

He had worked closely with Speaker Sam Rayburn in the congressional debate over extending the draft, a debate that was taking place just two months before Pearl Harbor. Then as a young senator after the war, Johnson was greatly concerned about the rapid demobilization of the armed forces which was occurring. During these same years he witnessed the beginnings of the Cold War, and watched with admiration as Truman instituted the Berlin Airlift and fought the Korean War. He had also been a firm supporter of Truman's aid to Greece and Turkey to combat communism, and he had backed the President on the Marshall Plan. In the late 1950's Johnson was a major force behind the probes into the nation's defense posture, and was a strong proponent of the space effort.[52]

Likewise, as Vice President, Johnson had had the opportunity to observe John F. Kennedy's leadership from close range. He had watched the disaster resulting from vacillation at the Bay of Pigs, and he had taken part in the tense deliberations during the Cuban Missile Crisis.[53] These two critical incidents in Cuba had made an indelible impression on LBJ's mind.[54] Kennedy and Johnson had a conversation after the missile confrontation, and both men agreed that forceful action had been the proper policy.[55] And while watching Kennedy's actions as President, Johnson had seen a President who believed his power to act was virtually limitless. Kennedy and his advisers had made the crucial decisions on the missile crisis entirely an executive prerogative, having had no advance consultation with Congress.[56]

Thus, to Lyndon Johnson, the lessons of the past seemed to point to the critical importance of national security.[57] Like few Presidents before him, he had a deep and abiding belief in the supreme importance of military strength for the insurance of peace. Johnson was keenly aware of what weakness and appeasement had led to twenty-five years earlier in Europe. He was determined never to let that situation happen again where the United States had any influence. So looking back over his shoulder, LBJ saw that the United States had been threatened by two dangerous waves of aggression, the Fascist and the Communist. The Fascists had listened to Roosevelt's critics, and did not believe that America would stand up for its interests in Europe. Similarly, Johnson believed the Communists of the 1950's had listened to Harry Truman's critics, and had thought that the United States would not defend its interests in Asia. Recalling all this, LBJ was convinced that the enemy assessments of American leaders had always been erroneous. Johnson, therefore, was determined to proclaim American interests loud and clear, and by deeds rather than by words.[58] In his memoirs, Johnson writes: "Like most men and women of my generation, I felt strongly that World War II might have been avoided if the United States in the 1930's had not given such an uncertain signal of its likely response to aggression in Europe and Asia."[59] Johnson was profoundly influenced by these memories collected over a long career of public service, and he steadfastly maintained that peace and freedom could only be preserved through overwhelming strength.

This kind of thinking was especially evident in Johnson's use of the "Munich analogy," comparing Communist aggression in the 1960's with the German aggrandizements of the late 1930's and early 1940's. The idea was not new. For instance, when the Communist forces of North Korea invaded South Korea in 1950, President Truman was spending a relaxed weekend with his family in Independence, Missouri. The next day he immediately flew back to Washington, but during that three hour flight on the presidential plane he had time for some serious thinking. President Truman later recorded in his memoirs the thoughts which went through his mind at that time. Most prominent in his thought process was the vivid memory of Hitler, Mussolini, and the Japanese Fascists, and how the reluctance of the democracies to stand up to this aggression at Munich had led to even more aggression, and eventually to World War II. Truman perceived the Communists now repeating that same kind of aggression in Asia, and unless the boom were lowered on them immediately in Korea, there could well be a third world war.[60] In the early days of the Johnson Administration, Harry Truman and the new Chief Executive had talked several times about the intervention in Korea. During those conversations, Johnson expressed complete agreement with the former President's analysis.[61] Writing in his own memoirs, LBJ noted: "President Truman gave me many good suggestions and wise counsel from his own experience.... He pledged his support for our efforts in Vietnam. He told me he had faced the same problems of aggression....He said that if we didn't stand up to aggression when it occurred, it would multiply the costs many times later."[62]

The impression made by the Munich analogy on Johnson was incredibly strong. There was a double confirmation of the whole idea, with Harry Truman recalling Munich, and Lyndon Johnson recalling Munich and Harry Truman's action in Korea. To Johnson, these experiences now took on the clear and unmistakable aspect of an historical parallel, a tempting guide for future policy.[63] Indoctrinated with this simplistic view of history, Ho Chi Minh became to Johnson another Adolf Hitler, a man bent on aggression, and if he were not halted it would be the old Munich appeasement all over again.[64] But President Johnson was determined not to have any repeats of Neville Chamberlain's performance, once declaring emphatically, "No more Munichs."[65]

This view of the past became an obsession with Johnson, repeating it to his staff and to those who came to visit him in the Oval Office. He would tell them about the ordeals of Roosevelt and Truman, and about John Kennedy's trials and tribulations during the missile affair. "The road to peace is not through weakness," he told them over and over. "Appeasement would be disaster."[66] Henry Graff has recalled a conversation he had with Johnson, and he remembers that the World War II analogy was one of LBJ's favorites. Graff writes: "Once more, the President talked about the coming of the Second World War, and how 'we had to stop Hitler even though many people thought we could be Fortress America.'" Graff recounts that Johnson made an obvious reference to Senator J. William Fulbright, the intellectual chairman of the Senate Foreign Relations Committee and a leading critic of the Vietnam War, when he stated: "Oxford didn't recognize the danger till the Battle of Britain."[67]

The need to stand firm in the face of aggression and avoid the disastrous mistakes of the past are seen time and again in the public words of Lyndon Johnson. In a statement by the President on Vietnam, April 17, 1965, Johnson said that Americans must protect their future against domination, conquest, and aggression--the "relics of a bloody past."[68] The same idea was expressed in the President's news conference on July 28, 1965, when Johnson answered a question about why the United States was in Vietnam. LBJ replied that three times in his lifetime-- the two World Wars and Korea--Americans had gone to far lands to fight for freedom. Americans had learned at a terrible and brutal cost, said Johnson, that retreat does not bring safety and weakness does not bring peace. The President declared that United States power was therefore very vital. Surrender in Vietnam, he observed, would not assure peace. He told the newsmen that the nation had learned from Hitler at Munich that success only feeds the appetite of aggression.[69] And again, this time in his State of the Union Message of January 10, 1967, Johnson compared Communist aggression with that of the Nazis. The President stated: "You will remember that we stood in Western Europe 20 years ago. Is there anyone in this chamber tonight who doubts that the course of freedom was not changed for the better because of the courage of that stand?"[70]

Lyndon Johnson, then, thought in analogies--to another Munich, another Korea, or another Cuba.[71] Yet, thinking in analogies can be a very deceptive and very dangerous endeavor. No matter how interesting it may be to draw historical parallels, it must always be kept in mind that no two historical events are ever exactly the same, because each occurs in a different and unique milieu. Despite arresting degrees of similarity, the exact time and set of circumstances inherent in two historical happenings cannot be precisely matched. The Cuban Missile Crisis is an excellent case in point. Writing about the dangers of historical analogies, the noted historian Arthur M. Schlesinger, Jr., remarks that President Kennedy had not over-emphasized the significance of his victory in the missile crisis. He privately expressed anxiety over the possibility of other people concluding from his success that the only way to deal with the Communists was through hard-nosed firmness and toughness. This worried Kennedy because he realized that he had had certain distinct advantages in that contest--it occurred in an area where the United States had local conventional superiority, in an affair where the national security of the Soviets was not directly at stake, and it put the Soviet Union in a bad light on the stage of world opinion. But JFK knew he had been fortunate; those same conditions, considerations, and circumstances might not exist the next time.[72] Another example was the drastic transformation of the Cold War which had occurred by 1965. Unlike the tense days during the late 1940's and the early 1950's, the NATO alliance had provided a strong military balance in the center of Europe, a Sino-Soviet rupture had taken place, there had been a lessening of Soviet domination in Eastern Europe, and the emergence of some sixty small ex-colonies into nations had put into existence new centers of political initiative. All this indicated that the world could no longer be conveniently viewed in terms of the Free World and the Communist Bloc.[73]

However, these were changes and modifications which Johnson and his advisers failed to perceive. Lyndon Johnson had arrived at political maturity during the late 1930's, a time when the threat of Fascist power stalked the world. No sooner was this specter obliterated then the menace of Russian power appeared. From the time Johnson was elected to the House in 1937 until he assumed the Presidency in 1963, there was not a single significant span of time when the democratic nations were not threatened from somewhere. There were no doubts in his mind about the evil of communism nor about the aggressiveness of the Soviets and the Chinese.[74] Johnson and those around him had been schooled in the foreign policy of Franklin Roosevelt and Harry Truman, and the lessons were hard to forget. They had been taught the importance of firmness in handling international relations, and they had learned that the high price of uncontested aggression would be exacted from all peaceful nations in the long run.[75] Johnson recited these lessons in a speech of February 17, 1968. On that occasion the President asked: "When men cry, 'Peace,' do they not know that Americans cannot give peace to the world by ever abandoning it to aggressors? When men cry 'Peace,' do they not understand that we cannot keep peace for ourselves by withdrawing from the challenges that the enemies of peace present?"[76] These convictions were held so firmly by Johnson that he was capable of stating on another occasion that if "we don't stop the Reds in South Vietnam, tomorrow they will be in Hawaii, and the next week they will be in San Francisco."[77]

Before leaving the subject of Lyndon Johnson's past experience and his tendency toward the employment of historical analogies, there should be mentioned another possible motive for his actions in regard to Vietnam. This is the idea that perhaps Johnson was attempting to imitate, either consciously or subconsciously, his old idol and mentor Franklin Delano Roosevelt. While this is undoubtedly the weakest of any credible Johnson motivations, there are still enough fascinating elements in the theory to justify at least a cursory examination of the subject. LBJ's trusted presidential aide, Bill Moyers, once said that Johnson was not a reader of books, pointing out that the President had learned mainly from history, and especially the years from 1933 to 1945, the Roosevelt era. Moyers admitted that for Lyndon Johnson, "Roosevelt is a book to be studied, restudied, and reread." The President had said on many occasions that "FDR was a second Daddy to me."[78]

Lyndon Johnson was a man anxiously concerned about his future place in the annals of history. It will be recalled that Johnson took great satisfaction in comparing his trials and hardships with those of the immortal Lincoln. But if LBJ wished to rank with Lincoln, he also had a great and overriding desire to have it recorded in the history books that he had equaled, or surpassed, the achievements of Franklin D. Roosevelt, a man he often referred to as "one of the giants of all times."[79] Johnson once candidly remarked: "I readily admit that my own course in life has been influenced by none such as this great man."[80] LBJ's aides were convinced that Franklin Roosevelt was the President's model and prime example. Johnson himself informed an interviewer that Roosevelt's portrait was prominently displayed on the wall opposite his chair in the Cabinet Room. He was tremendously impressed with FDR's tenacity and determination once a decision was made, traits which Johnson would later come to typify.[81] There were other similarities, too. Roosevelt, like Johnson thirty years later, inaugurated a sweeping domestic social program. In FDR's case it was the New Deal, and for LBJ it was the Great Society. But then after initiating that ambitious program, Roosevelt switched to foreign affairs and the waging of war, the change from "Dr. New Deal" to "Dr. Win the War."[82] This experience was also repeated by Johnson, whose "Great Society" endeavors eventually were lost sight of in the dense and seemingly endless jungles of Vietnam. And finally, in the opinion of many observers, it was Franklin Roosevelt who made the mold for sliding the country into war through devious maneuvers, an accusation hurled at FDR following Pearl Harbor and LBJ in the wake of the Tonkin Gulf episode.[83]

These then have been some of the many opinions and explanations put forth to account for the behavior of Lyndon B. Johnson as Commander in Chief. Some are rather convincing, others are somewhat tenuous, and still others are interesting. However, despite the plethora of print expended in support of one argument or another, there has not been any broad, all-encompassing interpretation suggested, an interpretation which would go far to account for the many varied and disparate features of Johnson's deeds and behavior. It is the opinion of this author that too many times the fact of Lyndon Johnson being a Southerner has been overlooked, or at least, minimized as a factor in determining his thinking and actions. One cannot understand Johnson without understanding the region he was a product of. It is for this reason that we now turn to an investigation of the single most important influence of Lyndon Baines Johnson--the South.

CHAPTER THREE

FOOTNOTES

[1] Philip Geyelin, Lyndon B. Johnson and the World (New York, 1966), p. 73.

[2] Tom Wicker, JFK and LBJ: The Influence of Personality Upon Politics (New York, 1968), p. 206.

[3] Geyelin, Johnson and the World, p. 79.

[4] Lyndon Baines Johnson, The Vantage Point: Perspectives of the Presidency, 1963-1969 (New York, 1971), pp. 18-19; 12; 22.

[5] Ibid., p. 12.

[6] Geyelin, Johnson and the World, p. 71.

[7] John J. Pullen, Patriotism in America: A Study of Changing Devotions, 1770-1970 (New York, 1971), pp. 118-119.

[8] Wicker, JFK and LBJ, pp. 206-207.

[9] David Halberstam, The Best and the Brightest (New York, 1972), p. 425.

[10] Quoted in Ibid., p. 530.

[11] Johnson, Vantage Point, p. 42.

[12] Quoted in Halberstam, Best and Brightest, p. 298.

[13] New York Times, The Pentagon Papers (New York, 1971), p. 189.

[14] Ibid., p. 114.

[15] Charles Roberts, LBJ's Inner Circle (New York, 1965), p. 223.

[16] Henry A. Zeiger, Lyndon B. Johnson: Man and President (New York, 1963), p. 101.

[17] Chester L. Cooper, The Lost Crusade: America in Vietnam (New York, 1970), p. 224.

[18] Eric F. Goldman, The Tragedy of Lyndon Johnson (New York, 1969), p. 17; Clarke Newlon, L. B. J. The Man from Johnson City (New York, 1964), p. 9.

[19] Wicker, JFK and LBJ, p. 249.

[20] Townsend Hoopes, The Limits of Intervention: An Inside Account of How the Johnson Policy of Escalation in Vietnam was Reversed (New York, 1969), pp. 8-9.

[21] Ibid., p. 16.

[22] Milton Viorst, "Incidentally, who is Dean Rusk?" Esquire, LXIX (April, 1968), 180-181.

[23] Ibid., p. 99.

[24] Henry F. Graff, The Tuesday Cabinet: Deliberation and Decision on Peace and War under Lyndon B. Johnson (Englewood Cliffs, 1970), p. 84.

[25] Cooper, Lost Crusade, p. 254.

[26] Alfred Steinberg, Sam Johnson's Boy: A Close-up of the President From Texas (New York, 1968), p. 826; Hoopes, Limits of Intervention, p. 22; Halberstam, Best and Brightest, p. 162.

[27] Pentagon Papers, p. xiv.

[28] Hoopes, Limits of Intervention, p. 21.

[29] Quoted in Ibid.

[30] Goldman, Tragedy of Lyndon Johnson, p. 400.

[31] Graff, Tuesday Cabinet, p. 59.

[32] Hoopes, Limits of Intervention, p. 7.

[33] Pullen, Patriotism in America, p. 159.

[34] Goldman, Tragedy of Lyndon Johnson, p. 411.

[35] Ibid.

[36] Quoted in Richard N. Current, Lincoln and the First Shot (New York, 1963), p. 7.

[37] Ibid., pp. 7-8.

[38] Ibid., p. 8.

[39] Ibid., pp. 9-10.

[40] Ibid., pp. 10-11.

[41] Pullen, Patriotism in America, p. 45.

[42] Current, Lincoln and the First Shot, pp. 8-9.

[43] Pullen, Patriotism in America, pp. 36; 41; 114.

[44] Cooper, Lost Crusade, p. 411.

[45] Hoopes, Limits of Intervention, p. 100.

[46] Quoted in Ibid., p. 102.

[47] Johnson, Vantage Point, p. 531.

[48] Geyelin, Johnson and the World, p. 34.

[49] Hugh Sidey, A Very Personal Presidency: Lyndon Johnson in the White House (New York, 1968), pp. 214; 218.

[50] Harry McPherson, A Political Education (Boston, 1972), p. 107.

[51] Rowland Evans and Robert Novak, Lyndon B. Johnson: The Exercise of Power (New York, 1966), p. 14.

[52] Sidey, Personal Presidency, pp. 214-215.

[53] Leonard Baker, The Johnson Eclipse: A President's Vice Presidency (New York, 1966), p. 120.

[54] Kurt Singer and Jane Sherrod, Lyndon Baines Johnson, Man of Reason (Minneapolis, 1964), p. 323.

[55] Goldman, Tragedy of Lyndon Johnson, p. 381.

[56] Jack Bell, The Johnson Treatment: How Lyndon B. Johnson Took Over the Presidency and Made It His Own (New York, 1965), p. 282.

[57] Sidey, Personal Presidency, p. 217.

[58] Geyelin, Johnson and the World, p. 45; Goldman, Tragedy of Lyndon Johnson, p. 380.

[59] Johnson, Vantage Point, p. 46.

[60] Pullen, Patriotism in America, pp. 110–111; Goldman, Tragedy of Lyndon Johnson, pp. 380–381.

[61] Goldman, Tragedy of Lyndon Johnson, p. 381.

[62] Johnson, Vantage Point, p. 31.

[63] Goldman, Tragedy of Lyndon Johnson, p. 381.

[64] Steinberg, Sam Johnson's Boy, p. 761.

[65] Quoted in Goldman, Tragedy of Lyndon Johnson, p. 381.

[66] Sidey, Personal Presidency, p. 230.

[67] Graff, Tuesday Cabinet, p. 102.

[68] U.S., National Archives and Records Service, Public Papers of the Presidents of the United States: Lyndon B. Johnson, IV, Doc. 194, April 17, 1965, 430.

[69] Ibid., IV, Doc. 388, July 28, 1965, 794–795.

[70] Ibid., VII, Doc. 3, January 10, 1967, 12.

[71] Geyelin, Johnson and the World, p. 13.

[72] Arthur M. Schlesinger, Jr., A Thousand Days: John F. Kennedy in the White House (Boston, 1965), p. 768.

[73] Hoopes, Limits of Intervention, pp. 9–12.

[74] McPherson, A Political Education, p. 445.

[75] Graff, Tuesday Cabinet, p. 181.

[76] Public Papers, IX, Doc. 8, February 17, 1968, 240–241.

[77] Quoted in Geyelin, Johnson and the World, p. 20.

[78] Graff, Tuesday Cabinet, p. 52.

[79] Bell, Johnson Treatment, p. 283.

[80] Quoted in Ibid.

[81] Graff, Tuesday Cabinet, p. 57.

[82] Joseph Kraft, *Profiles in Power: A Washington Insight* (New York, 1966), p. 156.

[83] William Appleman Williams, "Ol Lyndon," *New York Review of Books*, XVII (December 16, 1971), 4.

CHAPTER IV

THE SOUTHERN MILITARY TRADITION

No other area or region of the United States has drawn
more attention from historians than the South. Historical
scholars and various observers have frequently insisted upon
attributing an "image" or "central theme" to the Southern experience; but few have been able to agree upon what that image
or central theme was, or is. In actuality, the Southland has
provided scholars with many images, and as a result, the
definitions of Dixie have varied greatly. Making the problem
even more difficult, the South has often presented dual images.
On the one hand there has been the old "moonlight and magnolias" view, one depicting a South of graciousness, harmony,
salubrious climate, and leisurely living. Yet, on the other
hand, this same region has frequently conjured up a vista of
hate, violence, cruelty, relentless acquisitiveness, and
merciless exploitation.[1] But despite the many and contra-
dictory views, the one theme that recurs time and again like
a haunting echo is the motif of violence. So strong has this
been, that a leading student of the region was moved to write:
"No matter the guise, one underrunning trait brands them all:
violence."[2]

This realization of Southern violence is by no means a
recent discovery. Throughout the ante-bellum era, many observers,
some of them Southerners, specifically noted the many phases
of life and culture in the South which indicated a tendency
toward extreme bellicosity and militancy.[3] For instance, toward
the middle of the nineteenth century a visitor to the region
referred to something he described as the "fiery blood of the
South," and another traveler expressed concern over the manner
in which "wild justice easily degenerates into lawless violence,
and a bloodthirsty ferocity is developed among the ruder members
of the community."[4] In regard to the Southern character, there
was general agreement on their extraordinary spirit and will to
fight.[5] A penchant for violence was one of the traits of
character most often attributed to the denizens of the South.
The reputation of the militant Southerner was so well established that many Northerners perceived the area as one vast,
rampaging panorama of gentlemen resorting to dueling pistols,
of sadistic masters whipping slaves, of flatboatmen fighting it
out in rough and brutal fashion, of mobs callously gathered for
lynching, of amusement-craving country folk assembled for a

bearbaiting or a gander pulling, of romantic filibusterers
seeking danger and adventure in the Caribbean, and of paranoid
communities severely squelching any real or imagined slave insur-
rections.[6]   And it should be noted that while Southerners vehe-
mently disputed many of the judgments made on their lifestyle,
they never resented the imputation of a martial spirit as a
prominent quality of their character.[7]

Nor should it be assumed that this pattern of violence ended
with Lee's surrender at Appomattox. Nothing could be farther
from the truth. In his study of the Southern mind, the
journalist Wilbur Cash made one of his most perceptive points
when he attempted to minimize the differences between the old
and new South. Cash cogently argued that "the extent of the
change and of the break between the Old South that was and the
South of our time has been vastly exaggerated."[8]   He goes on
to demonstrate that the mind of that region was continuous with
the past, a mind strongly shaped by the conditions of that
past.[9]   This was certainly the case with the violence trait.
Writing of the twentieth-century South, a noted scholar has
described the South as "that part of the United States lying
below the Smith and Wesson line," an obvious reference to the
ubiquitous habit of carrying firearms there.[10]   In fact, the
South has traditionally ranked first in such categories of
dubious distinction as the conveyance of concealed weapons, in
the practice of lynching, and in other varieties of homicide.
Just as in pre-Civil War days, the Southerner is still regarded
as being "quick on the trigger," and prone to a determination to
"fight it out." The carrying of a pistol as an indication of
manhood was so common some years back that one Southern attorney
general characterized his state as an "armed camp in time of
peace."[11]

That the Southern propensity for violent behavior continued
unabated into the twentieth century is strikingly illustrated
in the South's conspicuous employment of what has been euphe-
mistically defined as "the summary and non-legal execution of an
offender"--or more directly and distastefully--lynching. The
use of lynching was comparatively rare in the ante-bellum South,
being at that time much more common on the frontiers of the
West. However, following the Civil War, the custom was greatly
extended in Dixie. For example, almost ninety percent of the
1,886 lynchings that occurred in the United States between 1900
and 1930 were perpetrated in the South. The Southland was unmistakably the region where mob violence was most likely to
replace the due process of law.[12]

Another indication of post-Civil War violence was the
activities of the Ku Klux Klan. The Klan had originally been
established during the Reconstruction years as a social
organization for Confederate veterans, and branched out to

oversee the conduct of the former slaves and to stifle crimes against white people. Then a new Klan gained notoriety again after the First World War due to its endeavors to encourage "100 per cent Americanism." Despite somewhat different goals, both of these organizations employed intimidation and violence in the pursuance of their ends. In many ways they were attempting to function as a kind of extra-legal government. Likewise, because of the secret and covert nature of the Klan, it was rather easy for non-members to adopt their insignia and costumes while committing acts of violence, ranging from the harassment of labor organizers and Communists to the direct commission of murder.[13]

Yet another significant illustration of the South's pattern of violence can be found in the number of individual homicides. Until very recently, it was frequently asserted that the murder capital of the country moved annually from one Southern city to another. This rather cynical appraisal of the situation does have considerable basis in fact, and even more importantly, gives powerful evidence of a continuing indifference to violent acts.[14] For example, during the five year interval between 1920 and 1924, the homicide rate per 100,000 population was somewhat over two and a half times greater than for the rest of the nation. The South was clearly the region where murder and manslaughter were most prevalent.[15] A study completed in 1938 found that the incidence of homicide was heavily concentrated in the states of the Southeast. In surveying the eleven former states of the Confederacy, it was found that Louisiana had the lowest homicide rate; yet even this lowest rate for the South was still 74 percent greater than the national average, and not one single non-Southern state had a higher rate. An interesting aspect of the survey was the fact that while murder and assault predominated in the Southeast, robbery figures were highest in the Central and Western regions. These discoveries were repeated again in a 1954 study, which employed the data on crime for the period from 1946 to 1952. The findings indicated high rates of serious crimes against persons in the South, and lower rates for crimes against property for the same region.[16] And a very recent inquiry into the situation concluded that violence in the South had three basic dimensions in relation to the North: high rates of homicide and assault, moderate rates of crime against property, and low rates of suicide.[17]

Thus, the most recent studies reveal that the traditional high levels of violence for the Southland have continued into the modern age. Why this should be the case has formed an enigmatic problem for investigators for a long time. The answers and theories put forth to solve this puzzle have been many and have been of varying quality. On one occasion a stalwart Southerner was asked by an inquisitive Yankee why the murder rate in the South was so extremely high, and the man replied that he just reckoned there were more folks in the South who needed killing.[18] As commendable as this answer is for its candor and brevity, it may still prove profitable to look at some of the other explanations for this most troublesome phenomenon.

One popular explanation for greater levels of Southern violence, and almost everything else, has been the factor of climate. The hot weather causes a resultant increase in volatility of temper and heightens emotionality. However, the plausibility of this interpretation is lessened by the fact that the number of slayings committed in December exceed those for any other month.[19]

Another standard explanation among Southerners is the extremely high rates of violence among blacks, the ethnic group which constitutes a large part of the population, and which could very easily raise the overall murder statistics for the South as a whole. The only problem with this thesis is that in reality there is a tendency for states with increases in the percentage of blacks in the population to rank lower in serious crimes.[20]

A somewhat more sophisticated theory contends that the white society of the South contains a larger proportion of lower status occupations. This means that the same variety of forces which causes lower status groups in the North to be more violent also has the same effect in the South. Nevertheless, this hypothesis runs counter to the Southern urban experience. In the cities of the South where whites show the usual pattern of Southern violence, there is actually a greater percentage of the white population in higher status positions than is the case with the Northern cities. So it cannot really be said that the class structure accounts for this skew in the statistics.[21]

Along these same lines, the agricultural nature of the South has been suggested as a possible reason for the distinctive pattern of Southern violence. Yet the evidence shows just the opposite. In fact, both homicide and suicide rates are significantly lower for rural districts than for the cities. Therefore, the unique configuration of violence in the South cannot be accounted for by rural living.[22]

Likewise, poverty has oftentimes been suggested as a logical factor in the deep-seated causes of the South's alarming levels of violence. But once again, poverty by itself is found lacking as a basic reason. The argument is seriously undermined by the general decline of homicides during business depressions in the United States. Another investigation into this matter discovered that there was no high correlation between crime rates and the percentage of a county's population on relief. This same study found there was, however, a high correlation between degree of urbanization and crime rates.[23]

Similarly, several observers have offered the explanation that the widespread habit of carrying guns in the South could account for so many altercations turning into murders in that region. This suggestion receives a certain amount of credence from the fact that the rather weak gun control bill passed by the House of Representatives in 1968 received an overwhelmingly affirmative vote of 304 to 118, yet the members representing the eleven former states of the Confederacy voted 73 to 19 against the bill.[24]

However, as the eminent Southern scholar C. Vann Woodward has observed, the outstanding studies of group or national character in recent times have been those which went beyond such things as circumstance, natural environment, and public policy. In his opinion, the better investigations have been the ones stressing _experience_ as the primary influence. The works which have focused upon the implications of experience and the way it is manifested in personality and group character, a concern with the public and external forces "that go to make up the collective experience and give shape to the group character of a people."[25] In speaking of the American experience, Woodward contends that a common history has not necessarily connoted a common experience, and he suggests that it has not meant a uniform heritage or character.[26] Arnold Toynbee, in the tenth volume of his monumental study of history, offers the theory that "the vividness of historical impressions is apt to be proportionate to their violence and painfulness."[27] The Southern experience offers an excellent example of the impact of historical consciousness.

Although a part of the total American experience, the Southern experience has provided some basic differences in certain particulars of that supposedly common heritage. For one thing, perhaps the most commonly mentioned American trait has been that of economic abundance. Yet the history of the South is replete with a long tradition of poverty. Another bedrock American characteristic often alluded to is the experience of success. But, conversely, the Southern past includes more than a modicum of failure, frustration, and defeat. Still another enduring national legend has been the myth of American innocence, the unique conditions of a New World beckoning and regenerating the men of a decadent and wicked Old World. Yet, once again, the experience of the South diverged. For a long time Southerners lived closely with the guilt and anxiety connected with the social evil of slavery, and lived through more troubled times in the aftermath of that institution. And lastly, there has been the popular generalization, first given expression by

Tocqueville, that the American was a man "born free." However, there were sizeable numbers of Southern Americans who were born into bondage.[28]

* * * * *

This influence of a distinctive past is best seen in the South's affinity for the ultimate manifestation of violence--war. The Southerner has long been recognized for his propensity to eagerly adopt the military life, and for the martial qualities which he has displayed in all the American wars. The profession of arms has traditionally attracted a disproportionate total of Southerners as career officers and long-term enlisted men, and the military vocation has been for the most part more highly regarded in the South than elsewhere. In fact, this penchant for militarism has created for the Southerner a niche in the pages of American history analogous to the position of the Prussian Junker in the German past. For instance, _Life_ magazine once allotted a sixteen-page spread to a feature which it called "The Fighting South," a title which had been borrowed from John Temple Graves' book-length study of the same phenomenon. It would be quite impossible for any scholar to prove that the Southerner in battle has been endowed with more courage or better fighting qualities than men from other parts of the country. However, from the viewpoint of statistics, it can be established that no other region throughout the American experience has sent its choice youth off to war so freely and so generously.[29]

The Southern past has been filled with many examples of an effusive military ardor and enthusiasm. For instance, it was in the South that the old and revered American tradition of a volunteer military organization or militia was accorded a most congenial environment in which to flourish. The militia muster and review became social institutions in that region, and very effectively aided in suffusing the martial spirit into the people who participated and attended. While local circumstances might affect the public attitude toward the citizen soldier, there nevertheless was a sizeable reservoir of respect for the military. The volunteer military organization and its warm popular support reflected the pervasive influence which the martial spirit had attained over many facets of Southern life.[30]

If the strong support for the militia demonstrated a Southern predilection for militancy and violence, the educational leaders and institutions exerted very little effort to discourage that trend. Free public schools were slow to develop in the South, and the ones which were established failed dismally in the endeavor to effectively influence the region's manners or morals, since some of the strongest demonstrations of the famed fighting spirit were found in many of the schools. In actuality, the martial spirit is well-evidenced by the remarkable degree of support in the Southland for military schools and colleges. During the ante-bellum years, Southerners gave enthusiastic support to the United States Military Academy, and to various attempts to found military schools in the South. In the three decades prior to the Civil War there was a considerable increase in the total number of military schools in that region. Although not all the ante-bellum efforts to establish military schools were successful, they were an important indication of things to come. These so-called "West Points of the South" were both a reflection of the martial temper and an encouragement to its continued growth. And the South still clings to its military traditions while its military preparatory schools still flourish. With minor exceptions, almost all of the essentially military colleges of note in the country are located in the South. The only two state-supported military colleges in the nation are found in Southern states-- Virginia and South Carolina. The Citadel and the Virginia Military Institute are but the outstanding examples of the firm conviction in the section that a military career is perhaps the most honorable one that a young Southerner can pursue. In effect, these military colleges are simply state versions of the United States Military Academy at West Point, and these state military colleges have contributed heavily to the officer personnel of the armed forces. In addition, the South contains a large number of private military preparatory schools.[31] All this taken together sharply underlines the tight grasp of the military idea on many Southerners. As one historian has observed: "The South, which of all the sections of the country has suffered the most from war, is the section laying the most emphasis upon military education; and this is due not to a fear of war but to a reverence for it."[32]

Along with this intense interest of the South in military education was the extraordinary number of Southerners who influenced national policy on the issues of defense and war. For example, between the end of the War of 1812 and the start of the Civil War in 1861, the War Department was directed by Southern leaders a great proportion of the time, and continuously between 1849 and 1861. Many of these Secretaries of War from the South were strong advocates for increased national defense. The eminent Southern statesman, John C. Calhoun, eloquently went on record for a bigger military establishment while he was serving as Secretary of War in 1818. Likewise, another South Carolinian, Joel R. Poinsett, was instrumental in building up the country's defenses during the presidency of Martin Van Buren. There was a great deal of public support in the Southland for a larger army. Many Southerners spoke out in favor of a stronger military force, and exerted considerable effort to see that the defense machinery was kept at a high level of efficiency. And not surprisingly, Southerners held almost every important position in the Army of the United States.[33]

This prominent Southern contribution to militarism continued into the twentieth century, also. The large list of national policymakers from the South who have been closely connected with war and defense would include such names as Woodrow Wilson, Cordell Hull, James F. Byrnes, Richard Russell, John Stennis, Walter George, Mendel Rivers, Dean Rusk, and of course, Lyndon Johnson.[34] During this same time Southerners still made up a significant part of the officer class of the armed forces. For instance, in the period between the two world wars, the fourteen states of the South which had been connected in some way with the Confederate cause, states comprising approximately 22 percent of the white population of the United States, provided one-third of the Army's officer personnel. And of these Southerners, there was an unusually large number of them in the high officer ranks. But by no means was this penchant for the military life confined merely to Southerners of potential officer status. In fact, when World War II broke out in 1941, the states of the South had by far the highest proportion of volunteer enlistments to induction than any other grouping of states.[35]

In this same regard, it is quite striking to note that in nearly every war of the United States, there has been a Southern-born President serving at the time and directing its destinies.[36] Thomas Jefferson of Virginia was President in 1802 when the United States took military action against the troublesome Barbary pirates. In the War of 1812, James Madison of Virginia sat in the White House, at least until the British paid a visit to Washington City. Then in 1846 when the Mexican War began, James K. Polk of Tennessee was occupying that office. Following this, the Kentucky-born Abraham Lincoln served as Commander in Chief during the Civil War. Moving into the twentieth century, Woodrow Wilson of Virginia was President when the United States entered World War I. Similarly, Harry S. Truman directed the American war effort in Korea. While technically from the border state of Missouri, the Truman family nevertheless was known to have sympathized with the Confederacy. And finally, Lyndon Johnson of Texas occupied the Oval Office at the time of the escalation of the war in Vietnam. In addition, of all the American Presidents born in the South, eighty percent had served in the military at some point in their lives prior to election. Conversely, when those born elsewhere are considered, it is found that eighty percent of those Chief Executives had no military experience at all. Finally, one might argue that the significance of the above is lessened somewhat due to the fact that a man from Arkansas, Senator J. William Fulbright, was one of the chief opponents to the Vietnam War. However, it must be pointed out that Fulbright was an intellectual and a former college president, not a common occupation for a Southern politician.[37]

Be this as it may, the Southerner's reputation as a fighting man rested first and foremost on what he had done during time of war. The story, like the tradition, is a long one, older in fact than United States history. It can be argued that the first battle of the American Revolution took place not at Lexington in 1775, but rather, at Alamance Creek in North Carolina on May 16, 1771. It was there that a group of farmers and backwoodsmen, known as the Regulators, assembled and protested the tyranny of Royal officials in the western part of that colony. The Royal Governor, William Tryon, was able to defeat the Regulators, and six of their leaders were hanged in nearby Hillsboro after a perfunctory trial for treason. One of those hanged was James Pugh, who while standing with the noose about his neck, declared: "Our blood will be as good seed in good ground, that will soon produce one hundred fold." Then, on May 31, 1775, after the news of Lexington and Concord, an assemblage of patriots in Mecklenburg County, North Carolina, met in Charlotte and drew up the famous Mecklenburg Declaration. This document contained a resolution to the effect that all the laws of Parliament concerning the American colonies were "annulled and vacated," stated that "no other legislative or executive power does or can exist at this time in any of these colonies," with the exception of that power wielded by the provincial or Continental congresses, it asserted that all the commissions from the Crown were "null and void," and categorically proclaimed that any man who would accept any such commission was "an enemy to his country," and it encouraged the citizens of Mecklenburg to choose military officers "independent of Great Britain." This Mecklenburg Declaration was adopted a full year before the rest of the colonies followed the example.[38] And after 1778 most of the actual fighting in the Revolution shifted to the Southern states. It was there that a Southern **gue**rrilla leader, General Francis Marion, performed in amazing fashion and won great fame as one of the heroes of the war. The British had called him a "damned swamp fox," a nickname which stuck, and he had fought very well on dry land, too.[39] No matter what observers in the North thought about the general subject of contributions to the winning of the war, Southern speakers and writers were nearly unanimous in their opinions. One of them, William Trescot, proudly asserted that the Revolution had clearly shown how proficient at arms the South was. He prophetically declared: "The military experience of the country points to the South as emphatically the region of soldiers...."[40]

The War of 1812 gave that region of soldiers a chance to perform again, and the South was more than equal to the task. It has already been recounted in this study how the young "War Hawks," from mainly the frontier regions and back country of the South, were determined to uphold the rights and honor of the United States, agitated vociferously for a large increase in the army, and voted overwhelmingly in favor of war against the British. President Madison finally gave in to this martial spirit and war was declared.[41] One of the most prominent of the War Hawks was John C. Calhoun. This young South Carolinian was elected to Congress in 1810, and became the chairman of the committee on foreign affairs, where he soon gained the reputation of being a super-nationalist. It was Calhoun who introduced the war resolution in 1812, and he worked so hard in the war effort that he was once described as "the young Hercules who carries the war on his shoulders." For many years he would remain a big army and a big navy man.[42]

There were three principal military campaigns which were conducted in the South during the War of 1812. There was a British incursion into the District of Columbia and Maryland in 1814, a campaign against the Creek Indians that same year, and the famous Battle of New Orleans in January of 1815. Likewise, volunteers from Kentucky served admirably in the American armies winning victories on the northwest frontier. Southern officers won their share of glory, too. A Virginia aristocrat named William Henry Harrison, former governor of Indiana Territory, was the commander of the American troops at the victory of the Thames River, an important battle taking place in lower Canada in 1813. Another officer from the South, Winfield Scott of Virginia, scored victories at Chippewa and Lundy's Lane in 1814, battles occurring just over the Canadian border not far from Niagara Falls.[43] And of course, the South produced the foremost popular hero of the war, Andrew Jackson of Tennessee. Jackson's approach to warfare was basic and direct: attack and hold your ground. Tenacious and tough, his own men would bestow the famous nickname of "Old Hickory" on him. With single-minded purpose he squelched the hostile Creek Indians in Alabama and neutralized the Spanish threat in Florida. But his greatest victory came at New Orleans in 1815, when his army of approximately six or seven thousand Kentucky, Tennessee, and Louisiana militia, along with some local pirates, completely smashed an invading British force of some 12,000 men.[44]

Following the War of 1812, Southerners flocked to Texas when revolution broke out in that territory of Mexico in 1836. Many of those who went there regarded the Texas Revolution in almost the spirit of a frontier frolic, and Davy Crockett of Tennessee would win fame and immortality in that conflict, as would Sam Houston of Virginia and Tennessee.[45] But the next real opportunity for the Southern fighting spirit came with the outbreak of the Mexican War in 1846, a war that would be begun, directed, commanded and mainly fought by Southerners. As has been previously noted, President Polk did not go into the war with a unified nation behind him. Yet, the states of the Mississippi Valley and Texas supported the war with wild enthusiasm. In all, the South provided twice as many men as did the North, with Tennessee sending so many volunteer troops that it was labeled "the Volunteer state." The war was dominated by Southern officers. The President had chosen General Zachary Taylor of Virginia and Kentucky to command the invading army. Winfield Scott, a hero of the War of 1812, was another Southern general of fame in the Mexican War. At the battle of Buena Vista a Southern officer named Jefferson Davis, a Colonel of the Mississippi Rifles, put his men into a V formation, which turned out to be a decisive move in the American victory, and Davis became known as the "hero of Buena Vista." A member of General Scott's expedition to Mexico City was a Virginian named Nicholas P. Trist, the chief clerk of the State Department. Polk had dispatched him with orders to conclude a satisfactory peace with Mexico at the earliest possible moment.[46] This meant that a Southerner would also eventually end the war. The fight at the fortress of Chapultepec, the key to Mexico City, demonstrates the dominant role of the South in the conflict. On the morning of March 13, 1847 the western face of Chapultepec was assaulted by General Gideon J. Pillow of Tennessee. Meanwhile, a Mississippi general, John A. Quitman, moved his forces against the southern side of the hill and cleared the approaches to the aqueduct. Following this, troops from South Carolina were the first to arrive, and not long afterwards the fortress fell.[47] Later, Mexico City itself was taken, Trist concluded his peace treaty, and the war with Mexico entered the history books shrouded with Southern glory.

It is beyond the scope of this study to recount in any detail the South's participation in the Civil War. The events of that war are known better than those of any other American conflict, and the heroism exhibited by men from both the North and the South needs no retelling here. Suffice it to say that the Civil War might plausibly have been avoided had there been lesser quantities of the old fighting spirit below the Mason-Dixon line. And almost certainly the war would have been over with much sooner had it not been for the inspired and distinguished leadership of Southern generals.[48] In addition, the experience of the Confederacy witnessed an ardor and a devotion on the part of many Southerners which has seldom been equaled; the Confederate cause was an all-out effort by both military men and numerous civilians, a cause filled with examples of unswerving loyalty and self-sacrifice.[49] After Grant and Sherman, the South knew better than any other section of the country the full meaning of war. Yet, the South's defeat in 1865 and the turbulent and trying years of Reconstruction did not really alter the old military tradition to any appreciable degree.[50] The memories of Civil War glories would do much to keep the South's militant heritage alive and well.

The Spanish-American War which began in 1898 was hailed by Southerners as an opportunity to prove national unity, as well as to demonstrate Southern patriotism and fighting skill. The war provided new evidence that a nation ruptured by the Civil War was now welded together again. The South reacted at once to the national excitement which occurred in the wake of the sinking of the <u>Maine</u>. The regular army's first concrete movement was the mobilization of men in Southern centers. Of the four major-generals appointed from civilian life, two of them, Fitzhugh Lee and "Fighting Joe" Wheeler, were veterans of the Confederacy. People within the country now felt a vibrant thrill of common purpose as the sons of Confederate veterans donned the blue uniform of the United States. When it was all over, it was evident that a sense of nationality had been found once again, one firmly grounded upon the twin realizations of national strength and unity. And the South gave its hearty assent and approbation to the imperialism which followed the war with Spain, too.[51]

The military amalgamation which had started during the Spanish-American War, when both Southerners and Northerners had fought together in the face of a common foreign foe, was brought to completion in the World Wars which came after.[52] Once the decision for entry into the First World War had been arrived at, Southern communities hurried to the support of such patriotic ventures as war services, bond drives, and many related functions. Also, representatives from the South backed the war staunchly in the halls of Congress. The influential Southern members who dominated Congress through the workings of the seniority system, and members from the region in general, put aside the old issue of states' rights and voted for the necessary war measures with nearly complete unanimity. On eight major pieces of wartime legislation—conscription, the Espionage Act, the Sedition Act, the Lever Food Act, the Railroad Act of 1918, the Overman Act, and the antifilibuster resolutions brought up in 1917 and 1918—the members who represented the former Confederate states cast a total of but twenty-one negative votes.[53] The Southern position was well stated and summed up by William B. Bankhead of Alabama when he declared in the House: "I challenge any lawyer here to produce a single judicial dictum that the Constitution...in time of war can stand in the way of any measures necessary for the saving of the life and very sovereignty of the government itself when in desperate peril."[54] And, as could be expected, America's great hero of World War I was a Southerner. Alvin C. York from Pall Mall, Tennessee, became the most celebrated American soldier of that war. The legend of Sergeant York began on October 8, 1918, while he was leading an eight-man patrol through the Argonne Forest area. On that patrol, York killed 20 German troops, captured 132 others, and put a total of 35 enemy machine guns out of action.[55]

Despite the conspicuous Southern contributions in the First World War, the outstanding performance of the Southern fighting spirit came in World War II. In that war, as in most of the wars of the United States, the first wave of bellicose anger came from the South. The Southland had despised Hitler from the moment he had started his depredations against the small nations of Europe. When war finally did break out in 1939, the region demanded that Britain be supported, regardless of any Nazi displeasure about it. In the crucial period from September of 1939 to December of 1941, the South ranked first in the Gallup Poll's regional list evidencing friendliness for the British cause in disregard of the consequences. For various reasons, while the crisis grew darker, Southerners scored consistently higher than other Americans in favoring measures to counter Nazi, Fascist, and Japanese aggression. Even before Pearl Harbor, people living in the South repeatedly showed up on the opinion polls as believing the United States would be drawn into the war, that American interests were tied up with the events happening overseas, that the country should give aid and support to France, Britain, China, and even Russia, that there should be a definite enlargement of the army and navy, that the draft should be employed, and that the neutrality laws should be repealed, or at least, revised. For example, in October of 1941 it was discovered by the Gallup Poll that while from 63 to 70 percent of the other regions felt that the defeat of Germany was more vital than staying out of war, the South as a whole registered a figure of 88 percent. And the isolationist group known as the America First Committee made very little progress in the South, even though they made persistent efforts in that area.[56]

This same Southern trend could be seen in the enlistment statistics. During the midsummer of 1941 the totals showed that Southern enlistments in the army and navy were well above the national average. Taking the nation as a whole, the proportion of army enlistments to inductions for selectees was 49.8. However, the figures for Kentucky stood at 123.4, with Texas at 98.6, Georgia 92.6, South Carolina 85.3, Florida 75.9, North Carolina 75.3, Arkansas 71.1, Tennessee 62.5, Virginia 60.9, Alabama 60.6, Mississippi 58.5, and Louisiana 43.9. Similarly, naval recruiting in the Southern states far exceeded the average for the country. For instance, the Northeastern states registered a total of 44 per 100,000 population and the Central states came in at 63; yet, during this same period the Birmingham district recorded a total of 121, Nashville had a 111, Richmond a 109, and New Orleans a 100.[57] The strikingly greater proportion of voluntary enlistments by Southerners before the draft was organized led Alabama's Congressman Luther Patrick to proclaim that "they had to start selective service to keep our Southern boys from filling up the army."[58] And as early as 1940 the Canadians were beginning to refer to their air corps as the Royal Texas Air Force."[59] "To Southerners, then," the novelist James Boyd commented, "Pearl Harbor was no shock; it was a relief."[60]

Nor was there any diminution in the Southern wartime role following Pearl Harbor. The first prominent American hero of the war was Captain Colin P. Kelly Jr. from Florida. Kelly was killed off the Philippine coast when he aimed the bomber plane he was flying at the Japanese battleship Haruna, which went down as a result of his brave act. Likewise, the first Congressional Medal of Honor in the conflict was posthumously presented to Lieutenant Alexander R. Nininger Jr. from Georgia. The Army's Chief of Staff, George C. Marshall, was a resident of Virginia and had received his military education at the Virginia Military Institute. Similarly, a general from Arkansas, Douglas MacArthur, commanded all forces in the South Pacific, while Admiral Chester Nimitz of Texas commanded the Pacific Fleet. And Harry K. Pickett, a brigadier general from South Carolina, was in charge of the U. S. Marines in the mid-Pacific.[61]

And not surprisingly, America's most famous soldier in World War II was, as in the previous war, from the South. Audie Murphy came home to the little town of Farmersville, Texas literally covered with ribbons. He had fought in the African, Sicilian, Italian, and French campaigns. Altogether he had amassed 14 medals, including the Congressional Medal of Honor, making him the most decorated combat infantryman in the Army. He earned his Medal of Honor for holding off, singlehandedly, an advance of 250 Germans. Murphy did this in France from the top of a burning tank destroyer, his clothing riddled with bullet holes and his trouser leg soaked with blood. However, Murphy's fire was so deadly that dozens of Nazis were killed and the entire enemy line wavered; the advance had been halted.[62]

Although the wars in Korea and Vietnam were not popular conflicts, the Southern military tradition was still very much in evidence. A Southerner, General MacArthur, commanded all United Nations forces in the Korean War until his removal by President Truman in 1951. Likewise, the commander of American forces in the Vietnam War was General Westmoreland, a native of South Carolina. And while there were certainly many stories of heroism in Vietnam, the general public was not really interested. The media, except for occasional Medal of Honor awards, gave very little coverage to the subject. There were no Ernie Pyles to record the courage of the GI in that war, and no Alvin Yorks or Audie Murphys emerged from it.[63] Perhaps it was in the very nature of that war that the one American soldier who did receive a great deal of publicity was being accused of war crimes. First Lieutenant William L. Calley was convicted of the premeditated murder of 22 defenseless civilians which occurred on March 16, 1968 in the village of My Lai. A resident of Florida who had attended Georgia Military Academy, William Calley was a product of the South.

* * * * *

How can this military spirit of the South and the fondness of Southerners for the military life be accounted for? Like most interpretations of such broad subjects as a country's or a region's unique characteristics, the reasons put forth to explain the pronounced militancy of the South have been many and varied. Some observers have cited poverty as a possible cause. This argument is based on the idea that since the South is the poorest of the regions, Southerners therefore had less to lose by war and were more willing to take a chance. Tied in with this theory is the notion that "have not" people are usually more inclined to belligerency than "have" people, while persons of comfortable circumstances generally do not want to fight. Others have pointed to the rural-agrarian nature of the Southland, implying that an agricultural people are more likely to stand up and fight for their rights than populations living in urban and industrialized areas. Still others, including the novelist Erskine Caldwell, have mentioned ignorance as a cause, since the South notoriously lagged behind the rest of the nation in the fields of elementary and secondary education. Closely related to this explanation was a comment made by a caustic critic of the region, H. L. Mencken, when he cited the South's susceptibility "for believing in bogus messiahs."[64]

Another popular explanation for the South's belligerency is the South's ideology of patriotism and loyalty. The kind of patriotism as exemplified by Virginia's Senator Carter Glass when he said of his own two sons in 1916: "I would rather be pursued through time and eternity by the pitiful apparition of their shattered forms than to see my country dishonored and its flag hauled down in disgrace."[65] Patriotism is a trait which permeates the Southern character. But, as in the case of militancy, accounting for this Southern patriotism is a difficult chore. On the one extreme, there are those who claim that it is an over-compensation for certain guilt feelings arising out of the fact that the South must go out of its way to prove its patriotism since it was the section which was once disloyal to the Union. On the other extreme, there are Southerners who attribute its origins to sheer virtue and superior character. The truth lies probably at neither extreme, but rather, at some point in between. For example, there is a strange and interesting connection between patriotism and religion. Both are devoted to certain symbols, such as the flag and the cross. Similarly, both have their rituals, sacred writings, hallowed grounds, and even music. Likewise, both patriotism and religion have heatedly disputed doctrines, and both are capable of generating a good deal of intolerance.[66] This phenomenon is especially vital in the present context when it is recalled that the South is the region of the country most vulnerable to the appeals of fundamentalist and evangelistic religions. Treating this point, an eminent scholar has written: "Even in Southern religious experiences, there was sufficient combativeness to suggest the presence of the militant spirit."[67] And Wilbur Cash, in his classic study of the Southern mind, saw patriotism motivated by fear of change. Cash writes: "The very passion for 'Americanism' in the South was at least in great part the passion that the South should remain fundamentally unchanged."[68] In support of that point a noted Southern scholar, Dr. Howard Odum, has observed: "Much of our belligerency is against those who do not believe as we do. It is defense."[69]

Yet, as interesting as some of the above theories are, none is really sufficient in itself to explain the characteristic Southern bent for militancy. Earlier in this chapter the point was made of how some of the better studies of regional or group traits have been those which emphasized past experience. Militancy, like so many other Southern characteristics, can be much more fully elucidated by considering several important and distinctive features of the Southern past.

A powerful and unique part of the Southern experience was what has been variously described as romanticism, or the feudal spirit, or chivalry. Some years ago a very influential book on the subject, by Rollin G. Osterweis, contended that the civilization of the Old South was supported by three legs--cotton and the plantation system, Negro slavery, and the chivalric cult. He argued that chivalric notions had a profound influence on the thinking of the region and went far towards differentiating the Southern states from the rest of the country. Speaking of the Southern brand of romanticism, Osterweis declares: "It helped to create a nation within a nation by 1860."[70] The South of colonial and ante-bellum times developed in the cavalier tradition. The fact that there were precious few actual gentlemanly cavaliers with high standards of living and general correctness of behavior is not the point. What is important is that they believed they were part of that tradition and acted the role, and that their fantasies and mores were borrowed and adapted for rougher usage by the other classes.[71]

The Southerner's penchant for romantic notions was stimulated by the lonely and dull routine of rural existence. The social structure of the South contained a complex of traditions which served to give that structure almost a feudal appearance. Such a structure encouraged a great receptivity for various chivalric fictions. Sir Walter Scott, the famous English writer of romantic novels, was a popular favorite in the Old South. In Scott's kind of romanticism there was an opportunity for the Southern planter to perceive himself as a chivalrous lord of the manor, and it could nurture in the smaller farmers a desire for themselves or their sons to eventually attain the exalted planter status. The ante-bellum plantation did indeed bear in many respects a striking resemblance to the medieval manor. The planter was endowed with social, judicial, and political powers in his neighborhood, and became the counterpart of the eighteenth-century English squire whom rich Southern planters strove mightily to imitate. Both were survivals of the tradition of the all-powerful lord of the manor idea from medieval times. Then too, the presence of Negro slaves added even more verisimilitude to the feudal image of the South. Because the Negro slave became a close counterpart to the serf of the Middle Ages.[72] In addition, the existence of slavery significantly contributed to the Southern relish for romantic inclinations. It had the effect of freeing the planter class from many of the more mundane and time-consuming drudgeries, and afforded that class the opportunity to read romantic literature and entertain romantic daydreams. It did much to foster an exaggerated pride in the ruling class, and imparted an almost instinctive habit of command beginning with the early years of childhood.[73] It also created what Wilbur Cash has called a "void of pointless leisure" for the poor whites who now disdained any so-called "nigger work." Instead, they became backcountry romantics, performing feats of strength and agility, taking pride in the large amounts of whisky consumed, gouging out the eye or similarly maiming a fighting opponent, bragging of being able to fight and love harder than the next man, and striving to eventually gain widespread fame as being "a hell of a fellow."[74]

Southern boys learned early in life the proficient use of firearms and other weapons. And once learned, everyday experiences kept the skills honed to a fine edge. Fighting became virtually a way of life.[75] Southerners tended to be hypersensitive concerning their honor. While honor was an intangible quality, it was still very real to the Southerner. He looked upon it as something precious and sacred to the ego, something that had to be protected at all costs. The elaborate etiquette surrounding the code duello is a prime example. There were definite rules and procedures for both issuing a challenge and for staging the encounter. A man of status just did not engage in a duel with a person who was not a "gentleman," such elements were disposed of with perhaps a caning or a horse-whipping. While many Southern states passed legislation against the practice of dueling, these laws were largely unenforceable.[76] For example, Benjamin F. Perry of South Carolina, the editor of the Greenville Mountaineer, once killed a rival editor in a duel.

But far from being troubled with any feelings of guilt or re-
morse, Perry could justify the act in these terms: "When a man
knows that he is to be held accountable for his want of courtesy,
he is not so apt to indulge in abuse. In this way duelling
produces a greater courtesy in society and a higher refinement."[77]
Thus, even though many high-minded men were fully cognizant of
the evils of dueling, they nevertheless would accept a challenge
in order to avoid the opprobrium of being called a coward and
thereby losing influence in society.[78] In the same way, President
Henry Noble MacCracken of Vassar College, when asked for a
theory about why the South was so eager to enter World War II,
replied that it was "chivalry."[79]

This apparent enthusiasm of Southerners to fight, whether it
was in a bar, in the street, or in more honorable dueling places,
can be largely attributed to the conditions of life which
developed in the South and which continued to prevail there.
The Southern economy, with its emphasis on large farms and
staple crops, hampered the growth of compact urban areas. The
Southland contained a sizeable number of the characteristics
generally associated with a rudimentary frontier existence,
such things as great amounts of uninhabited land, rough and in-
adequate means of transportation, and very few towns of notable
size. Visitors to the region almost invariably made mention of
its more primitive aspects, and many pointed to these as an
explanation for the South's unique features.[80]

So the South was a frontier. And the frontier was from
Colonial times onward a factor which impelled Americans everywhere to appreciate the importance of military organization.
One of the most significant aspects of Southern history was that
section's closeness to the frontier. This is not to suggest,
however, that frontier conditions of life were only to be
found in the South. Yet, the distinction here is that in the
North such conditions usually prevailed only in the new and
virtually unsettled regions located close to the frontier.
Because as these Northern regions grew in years and population,
there was also a growth and advancement in maturity and re-
sponsibility. But the Indian had been subdued and the pioneer
had pretty much disappeared from New England and the Middle
states before the settlement of the cotton belt had even really
begun. Likewise, in the South, even older and more established
areas persisted in the traits commonly associated with the
frontier. Meanwhile, the newer areas in the cotton and sugar
kingdoms fostered a frontier violence and militancy which became mainstays of the Southern scene.[81]

Violence was an integral part of the Southern frontier,
just as it is a natural feature of any frontier. The Southern
style of life was rugged and primitive from the very start, and
it remained primarily so throughout the rest of the ante-bellum

71

period. Although there was the introduction of the aristocratic
element and the country-gentry ideal into the life of the South,
the fact remains that the section was basically an agricultural
frontier. Wilbur Cash definitely emphasized the frontier aspect
of the South when he wrote: "It is impossible to conceive the
great South as being, on the whole, more than a few steps removed from the frontier stage at the beginning of the Civil
War." And another modern Southern observer, James McBride Dabbs,
has noted: "Parenthetically, Southern violence is also frontier
violence. The South has been and still is a frontier."[82]

The South's social organization was distinctly rural,
centering loosely about the farm, the plantation, and small
towns. The residents of the South were therefore, in actuality,
frontiersmen. Whether he be planter, overseer, yeoman farmer,
or dispossessed squatter, the Southerner had one basic re-
sponsibility--to guard and defend what they possessed against
various threatening and disruptive forces. As long as this
essentially frontier environment endured, the conditions which
nurtured crudeness and violence would also prosper. With the
very scant distribution of population over vast areas, and with
the virtual absence of any organized or systematic means of law
and order, men were of necessity forced to rely upon their
resources, a situation which encouraged an extreme brand of
individualism. In such circumstances, excellent ability with
arms and horses was vital. A Southerner could never be certain
that he would not be called upon to defend his life against
some forest creature or some hostile human being. In addition,
a great deal of the militance and violence resulted from an
adaptation of the code duello to frontier conditions, and from
this self-reliance demanded by the frontier. Personal honor
is more important in a sparsely settled rural area than it is in
the anonymous and faceless relationships prevailing in industrialized urban environments. Similarly, the proximity of Indian
tribes to the Southern settlements was another important factor.
It caused much anxiety and apprehension concerning hostile attacks. Even more distressing to Southerners than the menace of
the attacks was the presence of fugitive slaves among some of the
Indian groups. Likewise, in the early stages of the Southern
experience there had been a Spanish threat located on their
borders, another factor causing concern and uneasiness. And
so this frontier atmosphere did much to produce a tough, tense,
and sensitive fighting man.[83]

The case of Texas is probably the best example of the power
of frontier influences in encouraging violence and militancy
in a Southern state. The experience of Texas, besides the usual
frontier emphasis on self-reliance, included the threat of both
Mexicans and Indians, and Texans had learned early that they
could never afford to surrender. In any conflict with the
Mexicans, the memory of what had occurred at the Alamo in 1836

deeply affected their attitude. Nor were the Plains Indians a
foe to be taken lightly. These tribes did not know the meaning
of quarter, and they were devilishly proficient in the art of
human torture. So the Texans existed in an environment where
they were faced with two foes, to neither of whom could they
ever surrender--they had no alternative but to fight it out.[84]

It so happened that the military organization of both the
Plains Indians and the Mexicans relied heavily on horses. The
typical Texas border war was not an affair characterized by a
few pitched battles, rather, it usually consisted of sudden
attacks and rapid retreats over a wide front. The attackers
were always mounted, and their methods had the tactical
virtues of speed, mobility, and elusiveness. To meet such
threats, the Texans of necessity had to have a force of men on
horseback, and it was from these hard frontier conditions that
the organization known as the Texas Rangers emerged.[85] They
were just the answer; an observant writer once noted: "A
Texas Ranger can ride like a Mexican, trail like an Indian, shoot
like a Tennessean, and fight like a very devil."[86] Not surprisingly, the Rangers were a permanent feature on the Texas
scene by 1840. With their headquarters in the frontier town
of San Antonio, and led by Captain John Coffee Hays of Tennessee,
they did admirable service in protecting the region from
marauding Indians and plundering Mexicans.[87]

Another radical adaptation to the frontier environment of
Texas was the six-shooter revolver. Since all the combatants
the Texans had to face were mounted, it was essential for them
to have a weapon suited for combat on horseback, something with
a reserve power and continuous action. The man who finally
came up with such a weapon lived in faraway Connecticut, a man
named Samuel Colt. The close relationship between Texas and
its Rangers with the new revolver can be seen in the names given
to the early models. The first was simply called the "Texas,"
and the second was known as the "Walker," named after Samuel H.
Walker, a Ranger captain who had suggested certain improvements
in Colt's original six-shooter. And the battle of the Pedernales
in Texas may very well be the first time the Colt revolver was
employed against mounted Indians.[88]

So the problem of frontier defense was an acute one for
Texas. And Texas, the home of Lyndon Johnson, was and is a
martial state. The journalist William S. White once made this
observation about the Lone Star State: "They raise their share
of foolish men there, but the density of pacifists and
neutralists and conscientious objectors is as thin as the density
of cloud over Johnson City on a hot day in July."[89] Texas is
filled with various and sundry military installations. And
Lyndon Johnson's family tree was replete with men at arms, the

73

kind of citizen-soldiers who had habitually come forward whenever the call was sounded.[90]

The roots of this military tradition in the South, however, do not lie completely in the realm of Indian attacks and frontier militia-type organizations. Also very vital to that tradition were the twin factors of slavery and the plantation system of agriculture. Not only were black people traumatically affected by "the peculiar institution," but whites were deeply influenced by it, too. Certain basic evils were the outcroppings of the Southern productive system, including the Southerner's inclination toward unanalytical thought and impulsive action. It likewise promoted a violent streak in Southerners, an arrogant disregard toward the observance of the laws, and a distinctive attitude in regard to manual labor. And as noted before, it helped to imbue the Southern mind with a decidedly romantic and conservative tinge.[91] A perceptive Southern observer has noted this about the impact of slavery upon the South: "It is indeed, the base upon which we built our society. For we built it upon slavery, and slavery, however humanized by the grace of God, was established by violence and maintained by the threat of it. This was the smoldering volcano upon the slopes of which we built the Great Houses."[92]

So what the frontier had begun, the world of the plantation continued. It was an existence which was admirably equipped to preserve and even extend those frontier traits. For instance, one basic effect of the plantation system was to perpetuate the characteristic frontier conditions and environment long past their normal duration. The plantation system, by appropriating the choice lands into a limited number of large units, had the effect of discouraging diligent and ambitious immigrants from settling in the Southland. Instead of having the development of urban areas, the plantation centered about itself, a self-sufficient, self-contained, and socially independent little world of its own. Another crucial aspect of plantation slavery was the fact that the planters exercised almost total control over their bondsmen, a circumstance which went far to preserve the strong individualism that had grown up in the South. A great deal of stress was placed on the unrestrained satisfaction of personal whim, which led in many cases to a kind of pugnacious and surly kind of swagger. And finally, an institution like plantation slavery had the logical, and perhaps inevitable, result of contributing to a low evaluation of human life on the part of many Southerners.[93]

Another result of slavery, less tangible but still important, was the creation of a Southern self-consciousness. A self-consciousness originating out of the need to guard and protect a peculiar institution from outside threats and influences. The

Southern identify became linked with a cast of mind approaching a siege mentality. Although many identities go to make up the Southerner, they are perhaps most fully aware of being Southerners when they are defending their section against incursions from outside elements. Concomitant with this frame of mind was an extreme sensitivity to any criticism from beyond the South, and a marked propensity for rationalizing various regional faults. Southerners were becoming aware that with their lifestyle and institutions they were rapidly becoming isolated in the world community. They were the last defenders of an outmoded system, a system under increasingly persistent moral attack. All this helped to lead to the South feeling more and more insecure, and more and more convinced that enemies lurked on all sides.[94] This idea of the South as a conscious minority during the ante-bellum period was given book-length treatment by Jesse Carpenter in 1930.[95] Similarly, Frank Vandiver suggests that response to challenge is a constant theme in the Southern experience, a phenomenon he refers to as "the offensive-defense mechanism."[96] And this thought pattern continues to be prevalent in Dixie. The wrath that was once directed against abolitionists and the Union Army today is aimed at such things as civil rights agitators, the federal government, socialism, feminism, trade-unionism, Darwinism, communism, atheism, and daylight-saving time.[97]

And slavery certainly bolstered the military tradition in the South. The planter was the organizer and manager of a large agricultural operation which employed slave labor. These circumstances caused him to assume the role of almost a military executive. Because it was often desirable for the planter, and sometimes even necessary, to assemble a fighting force to insure that the slaves were always kept under control. It should not be forgotten that many Southerners lived in absolute dread and anxiety concerning the possibility of a slave insurrection. The South was living in an atmosphere darkly tinged with crisis. The nightmare of nightmares in that region was the stark fear of slave uprisings. So there was a definite concern over internal security, with Southerners perceiving an abolitionist behind every tree, and a slave rebellion always brewing somewhere. During times of uneasiness or apprehension, there were patrols which rode along the highways at night, saw to it that Negroes were kept in their cabins, and other similar efforts to prevent against any uprisings. Meanwhile, in the cities and larger towns there were special patrols used to police the Negro districts after dark. This patrol system had the effect of strengthening the role of the military in the South. In many cases there was a close connection between the patrol and the local militia. And the most powerful manifestations of the South's martial spirit would surface during times when there were rumors of revolt; one need only recall the mass hysteria and paranoia occasioned in the Southland by John Brown's raid in 1859.[98]

Another part of the Southern past frequently mentioned in efforts to discover the historical roots of Southern militancy was the period of Reconstruction. After the surrender of Lee's army at Appomattox, and with the end of the slavery era, the South was suddenly thrown into a time of social and political confusion. Great economic disruption had come in the wake of the plantation system, and considerable amounts of corruption and inefficiency characterized some of the new Reconstruction state governments. It seemed to many Southerners as if taking the law into one's own hands was the only solution on many occasions. There was an increase in crime and disorder, and the actual number of murders rose, especially homicide between the races. The old Southern custom of carrying concealed weapons was given a new life, and in fact, assumed the aspect of nearly a universal pattern of behavior.[99] Writing about Southern violence, Wilbur Cash has remarked: "In no other field was the effect of Reconstruction more marked."[100]

And lastly, despite the convincing nature of some of the above theories, it may well be that the best explanation for the South's militancy is also the most intangible. It is here that the immensely subtle, yet immensely important, quality of pride enters the picture. Like so many deep-rooted traditions of success, whether they be in the realm of sports, education, or perhaps culture, the military spirit of the South was self-perpetuating. The South enjoyed a high degree of success in military endeavors, and as a result, military events and heroes were virtually canonized in the region, to the unfortunate exclusion of noted contributors in such areas as economics, or law, or science. It is here, too, that one encounters the crucial importance of the family in engendering pride in martial achievements. The observation has frequently been made that nowhere else in the United States is so much emphasis placed by so many people on family history as in the South. The Southerner has often taken great pride in the achievements of his clan.[101] For instance, America's first publicized hero of World War II was, as mentioned before, Colin P. Kelly Jr. On the mantle of the little house in Madison, Florida, where Kelly grew up, there was an old musket. Attached to the musket was a plate which contained the following inscription: "This gun was used against the British in the Revolutionary War and the War of 1812 and was a menace to deserters and robbers in the Civil War."[102]

Thus, any analysis of the Southern mind must consider the factor of pride, and the singularly poignant memories of a lost war.[103] A respected Southern journalist once observed this about the teaching of history in the South: "They are still taught their region's tragic history as though it had happened

76

to a separate country."[104] A people's perception of reality, whether of past or present, is often determined by the myths which they incorporate into their lives. The defeat in the Civil War, and the humiliations of the Reconstruction period which came after, supplied a lush milieu for the growth of myths. One of the principal myths to develop was that which pictured the Old South through the rosy glasses of moonlight and magnolias. In this view, the plantation became a beneficent institution of kindly masters and contented slaves. Life was sustained by a strong and noble code of honor, replete with beautiful damsels and chivalric gentlemen. Such a conception of the past served as a powerful catalyst for an exaggerated, even chauvinistic, regional pride.[105]

But the most influential and persistent of Southern myths was the Myth of the Lost Cause. This myth, along with its many symbols, has flourished and prospered far longer than any other regional legend. The outward signs of this myth were everywhere evident in the South: the Confederate museums, the obligatory statue of the Confederate soldier in the countless public squares, respect and tributes for the Confederate veteran and his family, memorial and reunion ceremonies, devotion to the battle-flag of the Confederacy and the popular war song "Dixie," the walls of homes decorated with portraits of Lee, Jackson, and Davis, the naming of sons after the commanders of Confederate units, and the bestowal of political office to candidates who had served the Confederacy.[106] An important feature of the Lost Cause legend was the idolization and cult of the Confederate soldier. The Southern hero ideal became distinctly military.[107] The amazing growth of the United Daughters of the Confederacy during the 1890's is a good example, with two thousand local chapters eventually being established.[108] A journal, The Confederate Veteran, stated it all very simply when one of its contributors reverently asserted: "In the eyes of Southern people all Confederate veterans are heroes. It is you...who preserve the traditions and memories of the old-time South...the South that will go down in history as the land of plenty and the home of heroes."[109]

Boys growing up in that region were saturated with military lore, identifying with the immortal Lee, the great Jackson, and the dashing Stuart, imagining themselves dressed in gray, and charging the cannon's mouth with the battle-flag of the South held high.[110] Southern military exploits were carefully preserved, and were glorified in the retelling. Liston Pope, a former Dean of the Yale Divinity School, received his early education in the schools of North Carolina. On one occasion, when he was discussing the history textbooks used in those schools, he recalled: "I never could understand how our Confederate troops could have won every battle in the War so decisively and then have lost the war itself!"[111] Mark Ethridge, editor of The Louisville Courier-Journal, summed it all up succinctly when he stated that "our heroes in the South have always been military...."[112] In light of the foregoing, it should not be surprising that the big tourist attraction, the Disneyland of the South, is a military shrine--the Confederate war memorial at Stone Mountain, Georgia.[113]

In conclusion then, the South has had a violent past, a section which became noted for its militant tradition. The region had played conspicuous roles in all of America's wars, and had taken tremendous pride in the glories resulting from those conflicts. Lyndon Johnson, a native of the martial state of Texas, was a part of that Southern military tradition. The next chapter of this study will consider Lyndon Johnson the Southerner, and will examine the various influences of that heritage on his handling of the Vietnam War.

CHAPTER FOUR

FOOTNOTES

[1] David Bertelson, The Lazy South (New York, 1967), p. 101.

[2] Frank Vandiver, "The Southerner as Extremist," in The Idea of the South, edited by Frank Vandiver (Chicago, 1964), p. 43.

[3] John Hope Franklin, The Militant South: 1800-1861 (Cambridge, 1956), pp. vii-viii.

[4] Quoted in Ibid., p. 2.

[5] Ibid.

[6] Sheldon Hackney, "Southern Violence," The American Historical Review, LXXIV (February, 1969), 906.

[7] Franklin, Militant South, p. 3

[8] W. J. Cash, The Mind of the South (New York, 1941), p. xxii.

[9] Ibid., p. xxiii.

[10] H. C. Brearley, "The Pattern of Violence," in Culture in the South, edited by W. T. Couch (Chapel Hill, 1934), p. 678.

[11] Ibid.

[12] Ibid., p. 679.

[13] Ibid., p. 681.

[14] Franklin, Militant South, p. x.

[15] Brearley, "Pattern of Violence," pp. 681; 684.

[16] Hackney, "Southern Violence," pp. 906-907.

[17] Ibid., p. 907.

[18] Ibid., p. 908.

[19] Brearley, "Pattern of Violence," p. 685.

[20] Hackney, "Southern Violence," pp. 908–909.

[21] Ibid., pp. 909–910.

[22] Ibid., pp. 910–912.

[23] Ibid., p. 912.

[24] Ibid., p. 919.

[25] C. Vann Woodward, The Burden of Southern History, Revised edition (New York, 1968), p. x.

[26] Ibid., p. xi.

[27] Quoted in Ibid., p. 35.

[28] Ibid., pp. 25–29.

[29] James C. Bonner, "The Historical Basis of Southern Military Tradition," The Georgia Review, IX (Spring, 1955), 74; Hodding Carter, Southern Legacy (Baton Rouge, 1950), p. 62.

[30] Franklin, Militant South, pp. 173–192.

[31] Ibid., pp. 129–146; Bonner, "Military Tradition," pp. 77–78; "The Fighting South," Life, XIII (July 6, 1942), 63.

[32] Robert Douthat Meade, "The Military Spirit of the South," Current History, XXX (April, 1929), 60.

[33] Franklin, Militant South, pp. 214–216; Bonner, "Military Tradition," pp. 74–75.

[34] Pat Watters, The South and the Nation (New York, 1969), p. 369.

[35] Bonner, "Military Tradition," pp. 74–76.

[36] Ibid., pp. 75–76.

[37] Watters, South and Nation, p. 369.

[38] "Fighting South," pp. 57–58; John Richard Alden, The South in the Revolution, 1763–1789 (Baton Rouge, 1957), p. 196.

[39]"Fighting South," p. 59.

[40]John Hope Franklin, "The North, the South, and the American Revolution," Journal of American History, LXII (June, 1975), 17.

[41]Clement Eaton, A History of the Old South (2nd ed; New York, 1966), pp. 186-188; Bonner, "Military Tradition," p. 76.

[42]John Temple Graves, The Fighting South (New York, 1943), p. 49.

[43]Eaton, Old South, p. 189.

[44]Ibid., p. 191; "Fighting South," p. 64.

[45]Bonner, "Military Tradition," pp. 76-77.

[46]Ibid., p. 77; Eaton, Old South, pp. 331-333.

[47]"Fighting South," pp. 60-61.

[48]Bonner, "Military Tradition," p. 77.

[49]E. Merton Coulter, The Confederate States of America, 1861-1865 (Baton Rouge, 1950), p. 567.

[50]Bonner, "Military Tradition," p. 77.

[51]Paul H. Buck, The Road to Reunion: 1865-1900 (Boston, 1937), p. 306; William B. Hesseltine and David L. Smiley, The South in American History (2nd ed; Englewood Cliffs, 1960), p. 434; John Samuel Ezell, The South Since 1865 (New York, 1963), p. 333.

[52]Ezell, South Since 1865, p. 477.

[53]George Brown Tindall, The Emergence of the New South, 1913-1945 (Baton Rouge, 1967), p. 48.

[54]Quoted in Ibid.

[55]"Fighting South," p. 69.

[56]Ibid., p. 57; Graves, Fighting South, p. 4; Tindall, Emergence of the New South, p. 688.

[57]Graves, Fighting South, p. 82.

[58]Quoted in Ibid., p. 5.

[59] Francis Butler Simkins and Charles Pierce Roland, A History of the South (New York, 1972), p. 552.

[60] Quoted in Ibid.

[61] "Fighting South," p. 57; Graves, Fighting South, p. 86.

[62] "Life Visits Audie Murphy," Life, XIX (July 16, 1945), 8; 94.

[63] John J. Pullen, Patriotism in America: A Study of Changing Devotions, 1770–1970 (New York, 1971), p. 175.

[64] Bonner, "Military Tradition," p. 79; Graves, Fighting South, pp. 5–7.

[65] Quoted in "Fighting South," p. 57.

[66] Pullen, Patriotism in America, p. 16.

[67] Franklin, Militant South, p. 209.

[68] Cash, Mind of the South, p. 296.

[69] Quoted in Graves, Fighting South, p. 16.

[70] Rollin G. Osterweis, Romanticism and Nationalism in the Old South (New Haven, 1949), pp. vii; 9.

[71] Carter, Southern Legacy, p. 61.

[72] Osterweis, Romanticism and Nationalism, pp. 13; 15–17.

[73] Ibid., pp. 20–21.

[74] Cash, Mind of the South, p. 50.

[75] Franklin, Militant South, pp. 11–13; 15–18.

[76] Ibid., pp. 33–44; Eaton, Old South, pp. 395–396.

[77] Quoted in Eaton, Old South, p. 396.

[78] Ibid.

[79] Graves, Fighting South, p. 194.

[80] Franklin, Militant South, pp. 19–20.

[81] Ibid., p. ix; Bonner, "Military Tradition," p. 79.

[82] Hackney, "Southern Violence," p. 920; Franklin, Militant South, p. 24; Cash, Mind of the South, p. 10; James McBride Dabbs, The Southern Heritage (New York, 1959), p. 147.

[83] Carter, Southern Legacy, pp. 59-60; Franklin, Militant South, pp. 22; 25-32; Cash, Mind of the South, pp. 31-32.

[84] Walter Prescott Webb, The Great Plains (Boston, 1931), p. 166.

[85] Ibid.

[86] Quoted in Ibid.

[87] Ibid., p. 167.

[88] Ibid., pp. 167-170; 173-174.

[89] William S. White, The Professional: Lyndon B. Johnson (Boston, 1964), p. 145.

[90] Ibid.

[91] Bonner, "Military Tradition," p. 80; Dabbs, Southern Heritage, pp. 146-147; Eaton, Old South, p. 260.

[92] Dabbs, Southern Heritage, p. 147.

[93] Cash, Mind of the South, pp. 32-33; 42-43; Brearley, "Pattern of Violence," p. 688.

[94] Hackney, "Southern Violence," p. 924; Woodward, Burden of Southern History, p. 143.

[95] Jesse T. Carpenter, The South as a Conscious Minority, 1789-1861: A Study in Political Thought (New York, 1930), p. 5.

[96] Vandiver, "Southerner as Extremist," p. 47.

[97] Hackney, "Southern Violence," pp. 924-925.

[98] Franklin, Militant South, pp. 69-76; 80; 95; Bonner, "Military Tradition," pp. 80-81; Woodward, Burden of Southern History, pp. 53-54.

[99] Brearley, "Pattern of Violence," p. 689.

[100] Cash, Mind of the South, p. 113.

[101] Bonner, "Military Tradition," pp. 83–84.

[102] Graves, Fighting South, p. 86.

[103] Harry S. Ashmore, An Epitaph for Dixie (New York, 1957), p. 45.

[104] Ibid., p. 46.

[105] Paul M. Gaston, The New South Creed: A Study in Southern Mythmaking (New York, 1970), pp. 6–7.

[106] Rollin G. Osterweis, The Myth of the Lost Cause (Hamden, Conn., 1973), pp. ix–x.

[107] Cash, Mind of the South, p. 121.

[108] Osterweis, Lost Cause, p. 10.

[109] Quoted in Gaston, New South Creed, p. 172.

[110] Cash, Mind of the South, p. 121.

[111] Quoted in Osterweis, Lost Cause, p. 113.

[112] Quoted in Graves, Fighting South, p. 8.

[113] Watters, South and Nation, p. 201.

CHAPTER V

LYNDON JOHNSON, SOUTHERNER

Lyndon Johnson was a Southerner, a product of the people
and the land from which he had come. He was of the South, and
had a deep and abiding sympathy for its beliefs and its ideals.
Johnson understood Southerners, and they understood him. His
identity was firmly grounded in the attachments and experiences
of his early years in the South, to a greater degree than
almost any other national leader in modern times. Possessing
a fervent loyalty for his native section, he was extremely
sensitive about the criticisms directed toward it. LBJ perceived the people and events around him as a Southerner, in
the light of the lessons gleaned from his youth in Texas.[1] The
journalist Tom Wicker once observed: "He was and is a man of
the South in whom the heritage of Ol' Massa had been overcome
but not forgotten, as it never can be by any Southerner. He
was and is a child, too, of Texas and Colonel Colt, influences
just as powerful."[2] Johnson was indeed a part of Texas, his
roots were deeply embedded in its soil. He felt a special
identification with its history and its people. And Texas is
a part of the South.[3] Writing in his memoirs about his origins,
Johnson candidly recalled: "That Southern heritage meant a
great deal to me. It gave me a feeling of belonging and a
sense of continuity. But it also created--sadly, but perhaps
inevitably--certain parochial feelings that flared up de-
fensively whenever Northerners described the South as 'a blot
on our national conscience' or 'a stain on our country's
democracy.'"[4]

Thus, Johnson was by both blood and geography a Southerner.
This is especially important to remember because there had not
been a Southern-born President since 1921, when Woodrow Wilson
had left the White House a broken man. And no actual Southern
resident had been elected to the office after 1848, when Zachary
Taylor of Louisiana had accomplished the feat for the Whig
party in their last successful Presidential campaign.[5] Of
course, there had been a Southern President in the person of
Andrew Johnson, who had reached the office upon the death of
Abraham Lincoln, but that turned out to be a tragic interval
for both the man and the nation.

* * * * *

In reviewing President Johnson's genealogy, it soon becomes obvious that his line was unmistakably Southern. John Johnson, from Oglethorpe, Georgia and a veteran of the Revolutionary War, later had a son named Jesse. In 1846 this same Jesse, along with his son, Sam Ealy Johnson, who had been born eight years earlier in Alabama, took the wagon-train route to Texas. Once there, Sam Ealy Johnson in turn moved on to the hill country of Blanco County, still a wide-open and wild area, and still inhabited by hostile Indians. When the Civil War broke out, he joined up to fight the Yankees, and then returned to fight Indians. In fact, in 1869 Sam's wife Eliza, the grandmother of Lyndon, was forced to hide in the cellar of their little log cabin while rampaging Comanches ransacked the home above. She had a small baby in her arms at the time, and tied a diaper over its mouth to keep the child from crying out. After the danger had passed and she had finally emerged from the cellar, she discovered that two neighbors nearby had been scalped in the raid. Sam and Eliza were the parents of Sam Ealy Johnson Jr., the father of Lyndon Johnson. Sam Ealy Johnson Jr. would later marry Rebekah Baines in August of 1907, and the family of this woman destined to be Lyndon's mother was also very much Southern. Rebekah's father had been born in Louisiana in 1845. He spent his growing-up years in Texas and received his education there. When the Civil War started, he enlisted on the side of the South, and after the war worked as a schoolteacher, lawyer, and newspaper owner-editor, finally gaining an appointment as Secretary of State for the Republic of Texas. LBJ's maternal great-grandfather had pursued a career as a Baptist minister, serving in Arkansas, Louisiana, and eventually Texas. Later in life he gained distinction as President of Baylor College, and could count among his close friends the legendary Sam Houston.[6]

The Hill Country of Texas "is a stern adversary, giving grudgingly of itself only to the most determined. It is a land that weaves strong resilient human fiber, conditioned to adversity, grateful for good fortune."[7] These words of Governor John Connally of Texas describe the native land of Lyndon Baines Johnson. It was at those grass roots, in an area where the soil is dry and the sun is hot, that he gained his knowledge about life and about people.[8] The land of Lyndon Johnson had been American frontier almost within memory. Less than a hundred years before, there had been errant Indians stalking the vicinity.[9] Yet, if the frontier had receded in Blanco County, Texas, its legend had not. And the vividness of that memory was the heritage of every boy growing up there. Hunting and fishing came before baseball and football as basic skills in that environment. It was a region where toughness had to be demonstrated, at least through the mouth if in no other way. Tied up with this notion was the idea that a man must fight in some way to get what he wants, part of the

tradition of trouble and turmoil. Courage in a man is reduced
to fundamental levels, such as being able to stand tall and
stare another man down, to dominate and mold the things and
people around him, to speak and expect to be obeyed. Johnson
was fully imbued with those legends, and thus had a lot to
live up to. As President, LBJ frequently invoked the little
maxims and homilies which he claimed were pioneer axioms.[10]
This was true to such an extent that a respected journalist
was moved to write: "In almost every action that Johnson takes
today as President there is a strand which can be clearly
followed back to his home in Texas. As a branding iron sears
flesh, the memories of adolescence and early manhood in the
Texas Hill Country etched themselves on Lyndon Johnson's cor-
tex."[11]

When Sam Ealy Johnson Jr. had married Rebekah Baines in
1907, they went to live at the old family homestead. This was
a small piece of land located on the north bank of the Pedernales
River, in Gillespie County, near the communities of Hye and
Stonewall. The Johnson house was a low frame dwelling with a
porch running along the front, a typical rural Texas farm home
during the early decades of the twentieth century. By virtue
of good financial management, Sam and Rebekah were able to
adequately support their young and growing family. In this
respect, the Johnsons were neither richer nor poorer than most
other Central Texas farm families during Lyndon's boyhood
years.[12] In reality, despite the hard times during those
Depression days, Johnson was part of the Texas Hill Country
aristocracy. As mentioned previously, his grandfather had
played a big role in the establishment of Baylor University,
Johnson City had been named after his family, and his father
and grandfather had served in the Texas Legislature. This
meant that there was always a rich sense of family tradition,
and if there was not a lot of money, they still possessed land,
influence, and connections.[13]

Whatever his childhood circumstances, by the age of six-
teen he still had not found a goal in life, and so he went off
with some friends in an old "T-model" Ford to California.
When he came home nearly two years later, his hands as well
as his pockets were still empty. Finally landing work as a
shovel man on a highway gang, working from sunup to sundown for
a dollar a day, he soon grew weary of the drudgery. It was at
this juncture, after having a serious talk with his mother, that
he decided to go to college.[14]

College for Lyndon Johnson was Southwest Texas State
Teachers College. When once determined to obtain an education,
he progressed remarkably. For example, he finished his entire
college curriculum in just three and a half years, and this

87

included a year spent teaching an elementary class of mainly Mexican-American children in order to earn enough money to continue his schooling. And while at the college, he had the honor of serving as secretary to the president. Then, upon graduation, he worked a year as a high school teacher in Houston, and following this he was appointed as secretary to the recently elected Congressman Richard Kleberg. So in 1932, at the age of twenty-three, he went to Washington to begin a new and enduring way of life.[15]

Working as Kleberg's Congressional secretary from 1932 to 1935, Johnson gained his invaluable apprenticeship in the operations and workings of the House. In fact, he learned its politics so quickly and so thoroughly that he was able to win the speakership of the "Little Congress," an unofficial group comprised of the Congressional secretaries. This kind of ability and skill gained him an important appointment in the National Youth Administration as the Administrator for the State of Texas. So at twenty seven years of age he returned to his home state, and in just one year he had assisted some 18,000 boys in returning to school, and had helped 12,000 more get work on various kinds of government and private projects. It was his outstanding performance in the youth corps which brought Lyndon Johnson's name before the public, and which first gained him the attention of President Roosevelt, and paved the road for his entry into politics.[16]

It was in 1937, following two years as director of perhaps the best-run youth administration in the United States, that he sought election to Congress, running on a platform of complete support for the New Deal. Although there were ten candidates in the field, Johnson was able to win, and he began a long and distinguished career in Congress. Elected to the Senate in 1948, he became a leader in that body during the Truman Administration. During the Eisenhower Presidency he served six years as the Senate Majority Leader, and in that period he was instrumental in getting considerable amounts of legislation passed for the Republican Chief Executive. By 1960 he was ready to challenge for the Presidency himself, and although John Kennedy had emerged victorious, Johnson's fine reputation and strong position in the party earned him the Vice Presidency.[17]

But no matter how high Lyndon Johnson rose in national politics, he knew that there was a cruel flaw in his image, a flaw that was really nothing more than the accident of his birthplace and the society in which he was raised. He had an excruciatingly keen awareness of the widespread disdain and contempt of the rest of the nation toward the South.[18] One of Lyndon Johnson's old friends once speculated that if LBJ had

ever allowed himself a fantasy dream when a young man, his
fantasy would probably have been imagining himself the true
heir of Franklin D. Roosevelt; but when Lyndon awoke in the
morning, it was to the realization that he was actually the
heir of Huey Long. In such introspective moments he recognized
that he had sprung from a very different political ancestry.[19]

Lyndon Johnson had made the Senate function smoothly and
effectively while he had been Majority Leader, and under him
the Democrats had played a major role in the governance of the
nation, even though a Republican occupied the White House at
the time. But to Americans in general he was regarded as just
another politician, and a Southern politician at that. Johnson
knew only too well that he was considered first and foremost a
Texan in the minds of those who were familiar with him. He
was plainly cognizant of the fact that his Southern drawl was
not well received by many Americans. He had chafed for years
under the steady flow of criticism and mockery aimed at Texas
and the South, much of it appearing in influential newspapers
and magazines. And LBJ knew that all this was a serious handi-
cap to any potential Presidential ambitions he might have,
because it was an issue which other aspirants could exploit
successfully against him.[20] For instance, _Life_ magazine
wrote this about Johnson in 1956: "Johnson the candidate has
grave and probably decisive drawbacks as he, despite the hopes
of his supporters, well knows. He has little support in
organized labor. He 'smells of magnolias,' i.e., is a
Southerner."[21]

Dean Rusk once talked about the political problems presented
by a Southern accent. He noted that there were places in the
country which would accept almost any conceivable kind of accent
in the world, whether it be German, British, Russian, or Yiddish,
but still would not countenance a Southern accent, mainly because it is thought that anyone with such an accent is just
naturally a little bit stupid.[22] Sam Houston Johnson likewise
remarked about the drawback presented by his brother's region:
"First of all, he was a Texan--and that alone was enough to
curse him in the eyes of a vast number of snob reporters throughout the country. His accent, his manner, his country-boy candor,
all worked against him."[23] This regional prejudice haunted,
angered, and frustrated Johnson to such an extent that he
flatly declared in 1958: "I don't think anybody from the South
will be nominated in my lifetime. If so, I don't think he'll
be elected."[24]

Although realizing that the curse of the South was upon
him, Johnson did not give in easily, but instead, appealed
against the regional prejudice. Lyndon had started early in
his campaign to eradicate sectional stereotypes. For example,
in an editorial he wrote for his college paper in June of 1929,

LBJ declared: "Sectionalism is vanishing. Our nation is
becoming more truly American. One great factor in the wiping
out of sectional ties is the education of the masses. Our
colleges and universities are accomplishing a great work in
creating not Northerners, Southerners, Easterners or Westerners,
but Americans."[25] Yet, thirty years later such prejudices
still existed, and Lyndon Johnson was painfully aware that his
Southern image had done much to lose him his party's Presidential
nomination in 1960, that as a Southerner he had less chance of
being elected President than a Catholic.[26] But immediately
after receiving the Vice Presidential nomination, he continued
his crusade against regional hatreds. "This convention," he
announced, "has closed the door on the things which have
divided America in the past. We have stepped across boldly
into what I believe will be a wholesome, new day of hope and
harmony for all Americans regardless of religion, or race, or
region."[27] During the course of that year's Presidential
campaign he would repeat the same theme of ending regional and
religious prejudice over and over again. And he finished his
campaigning in Austin on November 7, just one day before the
election. On that occasion, he told his Texas audience that
"Americans are ready to lay aside the divisions of the 1860's
to meet the challenge of the 1960's. Tomorrow night the world
will know that the walls of the past are coming down. We're
building a prouder America where opportunity is open to all
regardless of their race, or their religion, or the region in
which they live."[28]

Nevertheless, no matter how much he might appeal against
regional prejudice, Johnson knew that it was still there and as
strong as ever. Even when he was picked for the second spot on
the 1960 Democratic ticket, he recognized that it was not really
a breakdown of such prejudice, rather, it was a confirmation of
the power of that very phenomenon. He was chosen because he
could help to heal a seriously divided party, and Johnson, with
his Southern support, could greatly strengthen the ticket.
Because only a Southerner on the ballot could calm Dixie's con-
cerns about a liberal and Catholic party standard bearer. It
was hoped that while Kennedy conducted a typically liberal
campaign in the Northern states, Lyndon Johnson could work with
the South and attempt to keep it in the Democratic column, a
strategy which worked well on election day and did much to
give the White House to the Easterner Kennedy.[29] A foreign
correspondent made this observation about LBJ and the election:
"He still believes that regional prejudice, in the 1960 election,
was more important than religious bigotry--that is, regional
prejudice stopped him, but religious bigotry didn't stop
Kennedy."[30]

And, if anything, his deep personal feelings of irritation
and frustration over the disparaging comments aimed at him due

to the region of his birth grew worse after he became President.
For one thing, the glamorous and popular John Kennedy was
murdered in Johnson's home state of Texas. This unfortunate
circumstance of geography was a bad start for the new and
relatively unknown President in the eyes of the world. "Texas
was always a joke," the British historian Denis Brogan was
quoted in _Time_ magazine as saying. "Now Texas is a bad joke."[31]
Johnson likewise was convinced that the Kennedy group and the
intellectuals would never accept him as President, they would
be after him all the time and would never give him a chance.
His speech, his personal mannerisms, and his Southern background, he felt, would prejudice him in their eyes. LBJ
believed that no matter what great things he might accomplish,
it would go unappreciated by the "Eastern crowd." He knew
that they were not happy about his being President, and gloomily
predicted that they would try to get him one way or another.
His education, he feared, would never match up to the qualities
demanded from Ivy Leaguers, and knew that his accent would
become a topic of derision in the stylish Georgetown salons.[32]
Frustrated to the point of near despair, Johnson once confided
to a friend: "I wonder if anybody with my background can hold
this country together."[33]

To make matters worse for the President from Texas, the
Washington press and officialdom are dominated by men and women
who are the products of the prestigious Eastern schools, and
this social elite has its own very definite system of courtesy
and protocol. In fact, it constitutes nearly a binding code
on the President, his men, and those who write about the
Executive branch.[34] For example, Johnson badly needed the good
will and respect of the White House press corps, but instead
they picked his Southern origins apart and labeled him "Uncle
Cornpone." Similarly, he needed the support of the commentators
and intellectuals, but with some notable exceptions it was
given grudgingly, if at all.[35] Reacting bitterly, Johnson
once told Henry Graff during an interview: "...Now they say
that I am not qualified in foreign affairs like Jack Kennedy
and those other experts. I guess I was just born in the wrong
part of the country."[36] Even cartoonists played upon Johnson's
Southern heritage. For instance, Herblock published a cartoon
in the _Washington Post_ of three White House staff members, their
bare backs entirely covered with stripes, groveling before the
bullwhip-wielding President. The cartoon was entitled "Happy
Days on the Old Plantation."[37] These were cruel jokes to a
man with an extremely sensitive regional awareness. The British
journalist Michael Davie perceptively observed: "The President
attributes the capital's rejection of himself to regional
prejudice. He thinks they don't approve of him because he comes
from Texas."[38] And even after he left office, he was certain
that his Southern origins, and not the war in Vietnam, had been
his downfall.[39] LBJ noted acridly in his memoirs that: "The

burden of national unity rests heaviest on one man, the
President. And I did not believe, any more than I ever had,
that the nation would unite indefinitely behind any Southerner."[40]

* * * * *

Yet, no matter how much he might rant and rail against the
invidious effects of regional prejudice, the plain fact remains
that Johnson did exhibit many typically Southern traits, and
did very little to hide them. For example, Lyndon Johnson did
act like the stereotyped Southern country boy on many occasions.
Theodore White put it mildly when he noted that LBJ's manners
"are those of the earth."[41] Not since Andrew Jackson, or
perhaps Harry Truman, had there been such an earthy President.
His personality was vivid and unique, the kind which invites
embellishment and exaggeration. There were certainly dazzling
abilities possessed by this man, but there was also sometimes
a definite uncouthness displayed in numerous personal traits.
As a legislator, polite Washington society had cringed when he
would spear meat at the table with an inimitable boardinghouse
stab, and throughout his career his manners were still mainly
country-style. Likewise, it was not unusual for him to pick his
nose during a meeting, or to slump down in his chair and
casually reach into his groin to ease his trousers. And on
several occasions the President insisted that certain advisers
go with him into the bathroom in order not to interrupt a
conversation, unashamedly performing the most personal of body
functions in their presence.[42]

Many of his gaucheries as President received widespread
coverage and publicity, and most of them involved true country
boy behavior. Many people were amused over the story of the
three New York broadcasting executives who visited the White
House with great solemnity for an important meeting. But then,
to their profound astonishment, the Chief Executive had
ordered them to strip and follow him into the swimming pool
after lunch, to participate in a new White House social function
called "skinny dippin." (There may have been a motive for
this, in that even the most powerful executive would find it
difficult to be pompous while completely unadorned in his
sagging birthday suit).[43] Then there was the very celebrated
tour of his ranch which Johnson provided for some Washington
correspondents. In scenes reminiscent of "Hud," LBJ packed
them all into white Lincoln Continentals and raced down the
highways at 80 miles per hour, all the while drinking Pearl
beer from a paper cup, hugging and embracing the female correspondents, and causing virtual panic among the Secret Service
agents. Similarly, there was the incident which came after his
gall-bladder surgery when the President lifted his shirt and
obligingly allowed the photographers to take pictures of his
barely healed scar. And there was the occasion when he picked

up his dogs by their ears, much to the chagrin of countless humane societies all over the country.[44]

But it was the mode and manner of Presidential speech which was the most distinctively Southern feature of the Johnson style. Like Huey Long, Lyndon Johnson had the knack of the rural Southern politician for employing barnyard idiom and vocabulary, a type of language which was earthy to the point of vulgarity.[45] For example, the President often spoke of "piss-ant correspondents" and their "piss-ant questions." When a reporter once began an interview with what Johnson considered a useless query, he said: "Why do you come and ask me, the leader of the Western World, a chicken-shit question like that?" His descriptions and definitions were often ingenuous, if not very inspiring. Speaking of a prominent official, LBJ once declared: "He can't reach his ass with his right hand." Similarly, Johnson once gave this assessment of the effectiveness of an international organization: "The OAS couldn't pour piss out of a boot if the instructions were written on the heel." Likewise, his definition of loyalty in an aide leaves nothing to conjecture: "I don't want loyalty. I want _loyalty_. I want him to kiss my ass in Macy's window at high noon and tell me it smells like roses." And his highly descriptive rationale for not ousting FBI director J. Edgar Hoover was unmatched: "Well, it's probably better to have him inside the tent pissing out, than outside pissing in." Finally, LBJ delighted the reporters on an occasion while he was still Senate Majority Leader. They had asked him why he had not taken one of Vice President Nixon's speeches very seriously, to which he replied: "Boys, I may not know much but I know the difference between chicken shit and chicken salad."[46]

Lyndon Johnson was also imbued with the traditional Southern conception of patriotism. His patriotism was of a firm and fundamental nature. He was a fervently nativist American.[47] Although patriotism is an extremely personal and emotional subject, a recent student of the matter has defined it as "love of country and readiness to act in its best interests as indicated by individual conscience and judgment."[48] Johnson had inherited from his own experience and from the history of his people a vision of America embodying a patriotism which could be both noble and chauvinistic. This is well illustrated by his behavior during the Dominican intervention of 1965. In the course of a speech justifying his intervention and outlining his peaceful intentions, he announced to his audience: "But if they are going to put American lives in danger--where American citizens go that flag goes with them to protect them." As he was speaking these words, Johnson swung around and jabbed his finger in the direction of a flag located behind the podium. Continuing with this theme, the President

was able to remember and recite a childhood oration, George
Frisbie Hoar's famous encomium to the colors. Said Johnson:
"As a little boy I learned a declamation that I had to say in
grade school. I don't remember all of it but a little of it
is appropriate here this afternoon. It went something like
this: 'I have seen the glory of art and architecture. I have
seen the sun rise on Mont Blanc. But the most beautiful vision
that these eyes ever beheld was the flag of my country in a
foreign land.'"[49] And it was difficult to argue the subtleties
of the incredibly complex Vietnam War with a man who perceived
of it as a defense of that flag in a foreign land. Lyndon
Johnson's type of patriotism was clearly evident in remarks
he once made about the war. The President declared: "When they
lead your boy down to that railroad station to send him into
boot camp and put a khaki uniform on him to send him some
place where he may never return, he doesn't debate foreign
policy. They send you to defend the flag, and you go."[50]

If Lyndon Johnson's basic patriotism was influenced by his
Southern heritage, then so was his love of direct action.
After several interviews with the President, Henry Graff
described his attitude in this regard as "cowboy style."
Elaborating further on what he meant by that observation, Graff
explained: "By cowboy style I mean what one learns early to
associate with the species: a preference for action rather than
the play of mind, a natural taciturnity, an inclination to
divide people into 'good guys' and 'bad guys,' and a practical
understanding of the uses and dangers of firearms."[51] Inherent
in Johnson's nature was a certain bellicosity, a conviction
that when confronted by trouble the best solution was to stand
tall, present a posture of strength, and not be afraid to use
force if necessary.

These tendencies gained from and conditioned by his boyhood
years in Texas come through clearly in several of the President's
favorite stories. LBJ once told a group of reporters that he
knew very well how to handle Latin Americans. Informing them
of how he had grown up with Mexicans, he described how one had
to deal with such people: "They'll come right into your yard
and take it over if you let them. And the next day they'll be
right up on your porch, barefoot and weighing one hundred and
thirty pounds and they'll take that too. But if you say to 'em
right at the start, 'hold on, just wait a minute,' they'll
know they're dealing with somebody who'll stand up. And after
that you can get along fine."[52] On another occasion, Johnson
recounted in a long story about how there had been a bully in his
school in Johnson City, who had singled out one boy in particular
to pick on. The bully would slap and kick him, but the other
boy would take it, because his mother had taught him that
fighting was wrong. However, the nice boy finally got fed up
with the rough treatment, and Johnson would delight in telling

what happened next: "But one day the kid decided he'd had enough. He turned on the bully, on the road home; he got him down and began to hit his head on the concrete, till his brains almost spilled out."[53] And another time the President detailed blow by blow the events occuring when a respected road crew superintendent brought Negro workers into Johnson City. Well, one day a troublemaker approached the superintendent about this, told him in no uncertain terms that blacks were not welcome there, and concluded his remarks by striking him on the jaw. Following this, a street was roped off and a big fight ensued, with the typical Johnson ending when the good guy "took both hands like this on the other feller's hair and said 'Okay, the niggers stay' while the feller's head was banging on the pavement. And there never was any trouble after that in Johnson City about niggers."[54]

And finally, Johnson was very impressed with another symbol of direct action recalled from his boyhood heritage--the Texas Rangers. While walking with some journalists one time, Johnson turned and asked them: "Know the difference between a Texas Ranger and a Sheriff?" When all had admitted that they did not know, the President enlightened them as to the difference: "When you shoot a Ranger, he just keeps comin' on."[55] And these were examples and lessons which could be applied in other places in other times. Perhaps to Lyndon Johnson the Vietnam scenario was just that clear-cut, with the Viet Cong representing the gun-slingers, and the first thing that had to be done was for the American vigilantes to clean them up and bring peace to the area,[56] even if it required some banging of heads on pavements.

An interesting element of Lyndon Johnson's penchant for direct action was his employment of the so-called "Alamo analogy." He had a tremendous admiration, even a reverence, for the Alamo, feelings which at times assumed almost the proportions of a fixation. As a boy, Lyndon and his friends often studied and acted out the early history of the Lone Star State in their games. A special degree of attention and emphasis was accorded to the glorious and tragic drama of the Alamo. Originally just an old Spanish mission in the quiet little town of San Antonio, it became the scene of the most amazing event in the history of Texas, when in 1836 a handful of tough and determined Texans fought for thirteen desperate days against a Mexican army outnumbering them 30 to 1. For young Lyndon Johnson, the contemplation of that heroic shrine became almost a religious experience.[57] Writing of Sam Houston's defeat of the Mexicans at San Jacinto shortly after the massacre of the Alamo, Johnson proclaimed in a college editorial of 1928 that it was a deed "so marvelously far-reaching and strikingly momentous that the whole world paused in astonishment."[58]

During his years as President, Johnson often made allusions to the Alamo in his public speeches and private conversations. For example, at the time of the crisis in the Dominican Republic, LBJ told the National Security Council: "It's just like the Alamo. Hell, it's like if you were down at that gate, and you were surrounded, and you damn well needed somebody. Well, by God, I'm going to go--and I thank the Lord that I've got men who want to go with me, from McNamara right on down to the littlest private who's carrying a gun."[59] Not long afterward there were twenty-one thousand Marines on the island. The Alamo analogy also proved useful in connection with the Vietnam War, the President drawing example and inspiration in difficult times from the steadfast and tenacious fighters in that epic struggle. When once asked to predict when the war would end, Johnson had replied in the true fashion of a man steeped in Texas lore: "After the Alamo...no one thought Sam Houston would wind it up so quick....Who knows how long, how much. The important thing is, are we right or wrong?"[60]

And perhaps the most famous gaffe of the President in a public speech involved Vietnam and the Alamo analogy. At the time of his first trip to Asia to view the military situation personally, he made a speech at Camp Stanley, Korea. The talk was delivered in an army mess hall not far from the demilitarized zone. The President was enthusiastically cheered by the assembled soldiers, and he was visibly moved by the experience. His emotions finally overwhelmed him, and after he had expressed pride in their dedicated mission, Johnson recalled for them some Texas history and his family's role in it. LBJ declared: "My great-great grandfather died at the Alamo," although in actuality his relatives had not even moved to Texas until ten years after that event. This was a fiction which would later cause the President considerable embarrassment, and many saw in it just another instance of the old Johnson "credibility gap." George Christian, LBJ's press secretary, later wrote that the Chief Executive had not deliberately fabricated the story, but had merely gotten his family history confused in all the emotionalism of the moment, and that he had really intended to mention his great-great uncle John W. Bunton, who was a genuine hero of the Battle of San Jacinto.[61] Regardless of the actual motive though, the incident demonstrates Johnson's tendency to exaggerate, and it displays unmistakably the power of the Alamo idea in the President's mind. He had grown up less than a hundred miles from that ultimate wellspring of courage, the names of its heroes like Davy Crockett, Jim Bowie, William Travis, and James Bonham glittered in his memory, and he longed for some blood connection to those paragons of bravery.[62]

Very much a part of this Alamo syndrome was Johnson's compulsion to act with courage. A persistent fear during his occupation of the White House was that future historians might write that he had not been a brave leader.[63] "I'm not going to go down in history as the first American President who lost a war," he had once emphatically declared.[64] LBJ possessed a tremendous respect for the old-fashioned kind of hero, and this facet of his character had a profound effect on his Vietnam decision.[65] "Just like the Alamo," he had said, "somebody damn well needed to go to their aid. Well, by God, I'm going to Vietnam's aid."[66] It is true that John Kennedy had been greatly interested in the chemistry of courage, but Johnson's brand of courage was the type which had originated out of his Texas background, the variety which still emphasized bullets, knives, good guys, and bad guys. There was a definite "Matt Dillon" streak in Johnson's character. For instance, in 1960 LBJ had informed Kennedy's press secretary, Pierre Salinger, to paint the Johnson image as that of "a big, tall, tough Texan." And it was this facet of the President's personality which caused much worry and anxiety in others, because many felt that it was too simplistic a philosophy of life for the modern age. As Commander-in-Chief, Johnson was in many ways a paradox. While running a mammoth war machine he also agonized over the billions of dollars which that war was taking away from his ambitious domestic plans.[67] But as a perceptive journalist noted: "At the same time he is deeply concerned that his courage might be questioned or that his resolve might be found wanting in the pages of history....that a Texan, nurtured in the idiom of the Rangers, might be called a coward."[68] Detecting this same crosscurrent in the President's mind, another correspondent wrote: "On the one hand, he would ideally like to do business with anyone. On the other hand, he is like a man on the frontier trail who feels that he must be constantly on the alert in case someone jumps him."[69]

A conspicuous feature of President Johnson's compulsion for proving his bravery was the habit of exaggeration. As mentioned before, when in Korea he had spoken of forebears dying at the Alamo. On a trip to Australia he had talked of fighting in the trenches there. A trip to Anchorage, Alaska, had resulted in a story of a dangerous flight there with Senator Warren Magnuson right after the Japanese captured Dutch Harbor in the Aleutians.[70] But the prime example of this tendency was his own wartime military career. When campaigning for reelection to Congress in 1940, Johnson had assured his constituents: "I love peace. I hate war. And if the day ever comes when my vote must be cast to send your boy to war, that day Lyndon Johnson will leave his seat in Congress to go with him." True to his promise, just one hour after voting for the declaration of war he volunteered for active duty and became the first member of the House of Representatives to don a military uniform.[71]

However, this apparently altruistic act was somewhat flawed by certain compromises. While he did volunteer for duty, he did not resign his seat in Congress. Neither did he actually enlist in the armed forces, rather, due to his political influence he was able to obtain an immediate commission at the rank of Lieutenant Commander in the United States Navy. This meant that he was spared all of the arduous and sometimes humiliating aspects of basic training undergone by the ordinary serviceman. And far from being put into a combat role, he was given a desk assignment in San Francisco, a job in which he worked with the United States-New Zealand Navy Command. Finally growing tired of that position, he went in person to the White House to request a more interesting job overseas.[72] Johnson received his wish when President Roosevelt appointed him as his special representative on a survey mission to the South and Southwest areas of the Pacific theater.[73]

Yet, here again was the type of job that only privileged persons with connections could expect to receive. Although it afforded him an easy and interesting tour of duty at very high levels, it also shielded him from any real danger. It was while serving in that capacity that Commander Johnson flew on a reconnaissance mission over New Guinea. The plane on which he was riding, however, developed a generator problem which resulted in a loss of power. Being partially disabled in this manner, the plane was fired upon, was hit, and eventually had to make an emergency landing back in Australia. Despite the problems, it had returned to base safely, nobody aboard the aircraft had been injured, and one enemy plane had been shot down. Certainly an exciting mission, but not really an extraordinary one. Nevertheless, Lyndon Johnson was presented a Silver Star, the nation's third highest decoration for valor, and it was bestowed by no lesser a personage than General MacArthur himself. The medal's citation noted that Johnson's "gallant action enabled him to obtain and return with valuable information." Then, after just seven months in the Navy, he returned to his seat in Congress.[74]

All in all, it was really a political decoration. But Johnson never saw it that way, and the event grew in importance with every retelling. As a matter of fact, following his accession to the Presidency he frequently displayed the Silver Star ribbon in his lapel. Likewise, just in time for the 1964 election campaign two aerospace writers managed to construct a book around the affair. Greatly embellished, their account argued that Saburo Sakai, the great Japanese ace, had been the one who led the attack against the plane in which Johnson was a passenger. But even in this very generous retelling of the flight, the only act credited to Johnson was that of occasionally peering through windows at the action outside, and the authors failed to mention what the "valuable information" was.[75] Be this as it may, the President progressively expanded this rather thin war record. Oftentimes when debating with Vietnam critics he would point toward his lapel, implying that his patriotism had been demonstrated under actual fire, and that it was greater than theirs.[76] And it finally reached the point where he could seriously remind Henry Graff in an interview that he, Lyndon Johnson, "had won a Silver Star in the Second World War for helping shoot down '20 Zeroes.'"[77] In a very critical book about the President, Robert Sherrill has suggested that there might have been a connection between Johnson's own dubious military record and his later extreme militarism, perhaps a strong drive to compensate.[78]

A very intense concern with machismo was a large piece in the Johnson puzzle. As President he had always been stalked by the gnawing fear that someday he would be seen as lacking the necessary manliness for the job, that at some critical moment he might be accused of being deficient in courage. Very insecure about himself, he tried hard to be constantly seen as a man. Machismo was something that he was very conscious and aware of, both in himself and the people around him. He needed and wanted the respect of those whom he considered to be tough, real men. Lyndon Johnson had unconsciously, yet invariably, regarded those around him as either men or boys. To the President, the real men were the activists, the doers, the kind who acted rather than talked, and who had the respect of other men. Boys, on the other hand, were perceived as the talkers, the writers, and the intellectuals, the kind who thought and criticized more than they acted. In this same connection, when Johnson analyzed the differing advice on the Vietnam situation he noticed it was the boys who were dovish and doubtful, and that it was the men who were confident and hawkish. Quite naturally, Johnson respected the men's advice more than that of the boys.[79] Being informed once that a member of his Administration was turning dovish, Johnson contemptuously remarked: "Hell, he has to squat to piss."[80] Likewise, Johnson was quite adept at chiding and questioning the courage of his critics, once describing them like this: "Most of them have set [sic] out all the wars. They love liberty but only talk about it. They have no style or character; they are uncouth and they have no guts...."[81]

To Lyndon Johnson, honor, force, and commitments were the important and manly things. He was a firm believer in the invincibility of American military might, of the concept of the frontier and the utilization of force to make certain that one was understood. He believed, in effect, all the images and cliches found in the myriad of John Wayne movies.[82] For example, during the Dominican crisis he had instructed McGeorge Bundy to convey this sentiment to the leader of the rebels there: "Tell that son of a bitch that unlike the young man who came before

99

me I am not afraid to use what's on my hip."[83] He faced a
world that he was convinced looked down on him, and he constant
tried to convince that world, and himself, that he was man
enough to beat it. So to Lyndon Johnson, the Vietnam trouble
took on the aspect of a personal challenge from Ho Chi Minh, a
testing of wills. He had to show his adversary that he was a
big, tough Texan who could not be pushed around, the kind of ma
who could stand tall under pressure. Talks and negotiations
could come later, what was important now was for the President
of the United States to demonstrate the country's strength and
his own mettle.[84]

Another significant aspect of Johnson's Southern backgroun
was the way in which it strongly influenced his relationship
with two of his most important advisers, one civilian and one
military. These two men, Dean Rusk and William Westmoreland,
would have a crucial effect on the President's handling of the
war in Vietnam. And both gained their powerful positions in
LBJ's councils at least in part because they were Southerners.

Dean Rusk came from a very humble background, being born
on a Georgia tenant farm. The son of a letter carrier, he grew
up in the Atlanta area. His rise to later prominence was not
the result of any family influence, rather, his career had been
advanced at opportune times by certain great patrons. For
example, in World War II General Stilwell helped him become a
staff officer in the China-Burma-India theater. Similarly,
General Marshall was instrumental in speeding up his rise in
the Pentagon and gave him his chance in the State Department.
And once there, men like Acheson, Levett, and Dulles aided his
advancement. Their influence also made him the head of the
Rockefeller Foundation, the job he held before being appointed
Secretary of State by John Kennedy in 1961.[85]

But as in the case of Lyndon Johnson, Rusk's boyhood in
the South was the great determinant of his later opinions
and actions. Even as a very young boy he was utterly fascinated by the military. During World War I, Dean and his
brother Roger carefully cut out the pictures of soldiers which
they would find in the newspapers, and would then paste them or
cardboard to make toy soldiers. They made thousands of such
miniature figures. Dean and Roger would also painstakingly
dig trenches as much as thirty feet long for their models,
and scrupulously followed all the battle plans. "There
wasn't a rich kid in town who had as many soldiers as we did,"
recalled Roger. And this interest in military things continued
for Dean. While attending Atlanta Boys High he participated
in ROTC for four years, becoming a student colonel and eventual
earning the command of all ROTC units in Atlanta. Another four
years of ROTC followed when he went on for a higher education,
with the result being that when he graduated from college it

as with a nearly unprecedented _eight_ years of ROTC training.[86]
Then asked to explain this one time, Rusk had replied in terms
of his Southern upbringing: "The tradition of the Civil War
was still with us very strongly...We assumed there was a
military duty to perform...We took that as a perfectly natural
part of being an American."[87] And Roger Rusk, a Professor of
Physics at the University of Tennessee, explained: "What people
also don't understand about Dean is how deep are his military
inclinations. It's part of our Anglo-Saxon heritage. The South
always had a military disposition. It's part of our stock."[88]

So it was not surprising that Dean Rusk and Lyndon Johnson
should become close friends during their years in the Kennedy
Administration. They had a common heritage. Both had begun
life as poor Southern boys who were ambitious, and many of
Johnson's relatives had originated in Rusk's part of Georgia.
Similarly, both men could point to Scotch-Irish ancestors, each
man had grown up with heavy doses of Southern white Protestant-
ism, and both men's grandfathers had fought for the Confederacy.
It was quite natural that they should be at ease with one
another. Southerners often regard Washington as a hostile
world, and they tend to be loyal to one another and protect
each other. They were two boys from the South, and Lyndon was
delighted to have somebody like Dean Rusk around. Observers
reported that when the two men would take a trip together they
were as happy as schoolboys, often speaking with exaggerated
Southern accents. Then, upon becoming President, Johnson kept
Rusk on as his Secretary of State, and showed a great deal of
respect for his judgment from the very start. And Dean Rusk
stood for a firm military prosecution of the war. So the
ideals and aspirations handed down to these two national leaders
from their forebears in the South did much to lend credence to
the accusation of Vietnam being a Southerners' war.[89]

If Dean Rusk was perhaps Lyndon Johnson's most trusted
civilian adviser, General Westmoreland deserves that designation
in regard to the President's military advisers. And among the
qualities which Johnson liked most about the General was that
he was also a Southerner. LBJ, already surrounded by Easterners,
could gain at least momentary comfort from Westmoreland's
Southern accent. William Childs Westmoreland was indeed a son
of the South. He was born to upper-middle-class parents in
Saxon, South Carolina. He had been born into a family with
tradition; ten ancestors had fought in the Civil War, and his
own father had attended the Citadel. It was no shock when
after graduating from high school, young William likewise
decided to go to the Citadel.[90] Then followed West Point, and
one success and promotion after another until he was finally
made U. S. military commander in Vietnam.

During those years as American commander in Vietnam, Westmoreland received more than his share of lavish praise from the President. In his public statements, Johnson expressed great confidence in the General, and displayed an eagerness to meet his requests. In statements at a luncheon for General Westmoreland in April of 1967, LBJ referred to him as "an exceptional and most remarkable American."[91] In his news conference of May 3, 1967, President Johnson described Westmoreland as "my best authority" in relation to the military situation in Vietnam.[92] In a similar manner, at a February 16, 1968 news conference, Johnson proclaimed that if he had to select a man "to lead me into battle in Vietnam, I would want General Westmoreland."[93] Likewise, on May 30, 1968, the President announced that Westmoreland's performance had been "exceptional and brilliant."[94] And finally, on July 12, 1968, during the presentation of the Distinguished Service Medal to Westmoreland, Johnson labeled him "a good American and a noble leader."[95]

Concomitant with this high level of respect for General Westmoreland was a fervent desire by Johnson to see that his requests were fulfilled. The General had the very broadest kind of freedom and discretion in developing a U. S. ground strategy in Vietnam. In fact, during the three years of combat and casualty escalations, there was no serious attempt made in the Oval Office to question or modify that strategy. It was Westmoreland's belief that the United States could eventually inflict such huge losses upon the enemy forces that they would come to regard them as intolerable, while U. S. losses could be kept within an acceptable range. As shaky as this hypothesis was, it was never really given any critical analysis by Washington officials. As it turned out, North Vietnam matched each American buildup in men and power. Yet, even then, Westmoreland was reluctant to have any change in strategy, and so a Southern President allowed his Southern General to preside over a bloodier and bloodier stalemate.[96]

And finally, the ultimate expression of the power of Lyndon Johnson's Southern heritage was his high regard for, and his constant infatuation with, the military. Most of his experience and interests as a representative and a senator were closely connected with the military and the more efficient conduct of war. The basic theme which recurs time and again in his public utterances was the conviction that there had to be a mighty military arm to support national policy. It was Johnson's frequently expressed belief that a President should have the very widest latitude in using his power, without any interference from Congress on matters of international re-lationships.[97] Dwight Eisenhower, in his book Waging Peace, made this observation about the man from Texas: "Senator Lyndon Johnson, on the other hand, appeared to be anxious to be able to take some action, visible to the world, to indicate we had...strengthened our Armed Forces."98 And when Johnson reached that office, he became probably the most militaristic Chief Executive in the nation's history. This was true to such an extent that a respected political observer could write: "Lyndon Johnson became, and remains to this day, a Big Navy man--and also a Big Army, Big Air Force, Big Marine Corps man."99 It should be remembered, too, that all of this was very congenial to his personality, background, and circumstances.100

    Lyndon Johnson's relationship with the military had been long and conspicuous. As a young congressman he had gained considerable public attention as a vocal member of the Naval Affairs Committee. His influence on that committee was heightened due to the fact that he got along very well with its Southern chairman, Representative Carl Vinson of Georgia. His performance on Vinson's committee was memorable, both for the firm manner in which he could manipulate witnesses and for the skill he displayed in bringing naval installations to Texas. For example, Johnson played key roles in having a gigantic Naval air training base located at Corpus Christi, in a Naval Reserve Station being put into the Dallas area, in the es- tablishment of a Naval ROTC unit at the University of Texas, and in the placement of large ship building yards at Houston and Orange. With the outbreak of war in Europe, the Texas congress- man was in the forefront of those warning that the country was falling behind in its preparedness program. And after the United States entered the Second World War, he was clearly one of the most enthusiastic congressional supporters of a relentless prosecution of the war. Johnson was indefatigable in his efforts and demands for more ships, planes, and military supplies in general, and he also accepted the chairmanship of a House sub- committee on the uses of manpower in the Navy. Then, immediately following the war, Johnson was greatly concerned that America was disarming too quickly, and argued that military strength would be vital in maintaining the nation's moral obligations in the postwar world. In short, he became the dedicated supporter and symbol of military preparedness in the House.101

    In 1948, Johnson was elected to the Senate, and he soon became there what he had been in the House, a noted leader in matters of military preparedness and collective security. Just as in the House, he served on the Armed Services Committee, and once again a Southerner, Richard Russell of Georgia, was chair- man of the committee and developed a real liking for Lyndon. Although they did not agree on all issues, both men were firm advocates of protecting the country through an overwhelming weight of arms. The chairman's own Georgia was so generously populated with military bases that one Air Force officer once jokingly remarked that "one more would sink the state." As a member of the Senate committee, he fought tenaciously for greater strength in the air, on the seas, and in the Army. With Russell's blessing and support he was able to propose the establishment of a Senate Preparedness Investigating Subcommittee, of which he was made chairman. Johnson struggled determinedly against President Truman's military budget, which he felt allotted too little for defense spending.[102]

Along with his belief in the need for more defense spending came a very real concern over the seriousness of the Communist threat. Communism for Johnson was a dark and monolithic force bent upon the destruction of the West and the capture of the world.[103] He once bellicosely declared: "If anywhere in the world--by any means, open or concealed--Communism trespasses upon the soil of the free world, we should unleash all the power at our command upon the vitals of the Soviet Union."[104] And with the outbreak of the Korean War, Lyndon Johnson became what Eric Sevareid described as "the people's advocate" for a vigorous effort, and called for a long-range global strategy for victory, and the immediate mobilization of manpower and economic resources.[105] He attacked the President's critics, telling them that the Communists, and not Truman, were responsible for the conflict. "The quicker we direct our hostility to the enemy instead of our own leaders," he said, "the quicker we will get the job done."[106] The senator from Texas called repeatedly for a national will to win. With the war over, his interest in defense and the military stayed as strong as ever, and he was now considered the conscience of the Senate when it came to the issue of national security.[107]

An interesting aspect of Johnson's concern with defense while in the Senate was his active role in the nation's space program. Following the Russian launching of Sputnik in October of 1957, Senator Johnson included space exploration among his ideas for national security. He was the principal organizer and first chairman of the Senate Committee on Aeronautical and Space Sciences. The National Space Act was drawn up by the committee, and it was that bill which set up the National Aeronautics and Space Administration (NASA). Johnson was a driving force in getting the Eisenhower Administration to speed up the missile program, and most of the key personnel involved later admitted that LBJ did more than any other government official in developing the American space program.[108] His brother Sam Houston Johnson was certainly of that opinion when he wrote: "I have always felt that Lyndon has never been given enough credit for his part in getting us going in space. It really should have been Lyndon's name they left on that plaque on the moon."[109] But Johnson's interest in space exploration for defense purposes led him to certain excesses. For example, on January 7, 1958, he told a meeting of Democratic senators that control of space "means control of the world, far

more certainly, far more totally than any control that has ever
or could ever be achieved by weapons, or by troops of occupation
...Whoever gains that ultimate position gains control, total
control, over the earth, for purposes of tyranny or for the
service of freedom."[110] The New York Times sharply criticized
Johnson for conjuring up such frightening images of a possible
American spatial imperialism, saying: "He is unquestionably
right in underlining the need for a major scientific assault
on outer space; but he is making a big mistake in couching his
plea in terms of unilateral American 'control of the world.'"[111]

Although he left Congress in 1961 to become Vice President,
his militant nature was still very much in evidence in that new
position. When Kennedy was making plans for a Vienna summit
conference, which did take place in June of 1961, Johnson had
argued against the idea, contending that the Cold War was a
permanent feature of the modern world, and that the only
language the Soviets understood was massive military might.[112]
Similarly, in relation to the Cuban issue, the Vice President
believed that the best solution would be a large-scale military
liberation of that island, declaring that "the only real way
to remove that threat--to cut out the cancer soon enough--
is to overthrow the Communist regime--and the only way to do
that is by invasion and occupation."[113] And in May of 1961
Kennedy had sent Johnson on an official mission to Southeast
Asia, a journey which included stops in South Vietnam, Taiwan,
the Philippines, Thailand, India, and Pakistan. Meeting with
Ngo Dinh Diem, Johnson referred to him as "the Churchill of
today," and promptly entered into an agreement with him for
increased American military assistance. He also mentioned to
the South Vietnamese leader the possibility of stationing
American troops in South Vietnam and Thailand. Thus, as early
as 1961 Lyndon Johnson was far from averse to the idea of putting
major United States forces into Southeast Asia.[114]

And after becoming President, although he did allow
Secretary McNamara to close down some redundant military bases,
Johnson's deep respect and concern for the military continued
with renewed vigor. The thirty-sixth President was immensely
proud of the United States military, and was eager to support
them in any way possible. His first public statement on the
military came just a few short weeks after the assassination
of John Kennedy, when he spoke at the Pentagon auditorium
before the Joint Chiefs of Staff and Defense Department officials on December 11, 1963. Said Johnson: "There is no
higher calling than yours, and none with greater importance for
the peace and safety of our country and the world." The
President went on to assure them that he would be faithful in
his support. "So you can count on me," declared Johnson, "for
the support that the Armed Forces of our country deserve at all

times."[115] Likewise, on January 20, 1964, the Chief Executive
stated that military men represented "the noblest and the best"
that was in America.[116] Similarly, his State of the Union
Message on January 12, 1966 contained the same strong commitment
to America's armed forces. The President asserted: "But we
will give our fighting men what they must have: every gun,
and every dollar, and every decision--whatever the cost or
whatever the challenge."[117] And again, in remarks made on
November 11, 1967, Johnson was hearty in his approbation of
the American military. On that occasion he stated that military
personnel were inculcated with the "finest ideals of this
Nation."[118] Finally, in another speech that same day, Johnson
referred to America's servicemen of past and present as "the
clay of our history," and "the fresh earth in which freedom
is planted and in which liberty grows."[119] The Southern
military tradition had reached the White House.

CHAPTER FIVE

FOOTNOTES

[1]William C. Pool, Emmie Craddock, and David E. Conrad,
Lyndon Baines Johnson: The Formative Years (San Marcos, 1965),
p. 181; Tom Wicker, JFK and LBJ: The Influence of Personality
Upon Politics (New York, 1968), p. 175; William Appleman
Williams, "Ol Lyndon," New York Review of Books, XVII
(December 16, 1971), 3.

[2]Wicker, JFK and LBJ, p. 252.

[3]Lyndon Baines Johnson, The Vantage Point: Perspectives of
the Presidency, 1963-1969 (New York, 1971), p. 155.

[4]Ibid.

[5]Wicker, JFK and LBJ, p. 152.

[6]Theodore H. White, The Making of the President 1964
(New York, 1965), p. 51; Kurt Singer and Jane Sherrod, Lyndon
Baines Johnson, Man of Reason (Minneapolis, 1964), p. 94.

[7]Quoted in Pool et al, The Formative Years, p. 1.

[8]Ibid.

[9]Michael Davie, LBJ: A Foreign Observer's Viewpoint
(New York, 1966), p. 41.

[10]Hugh Sidey, A Very Personal Presidency: Lyndon Johnson
in the White House (New York, 1968), p. 20.

[11]Ibid., p. 14.

[12]Pool et al, The Formative Years, pp. 49-50; 176.

[13]David Halberstam, "Lyndon," Esquire, LXXVIII (August, 1972),
81.

[14]White, Making of the President 1964, p. 37.

[15]Ibid., pp. 37-38.

[16] Ibid., pp. 38-39.

[17] Ibid., pp. 39-41.

[18] Richard Harwood and Haynes Johnson, Lyndon (New York, 1973), p. 55; Williams, "Ol Lyndon," p. 3.

[19] T. Harry Williams, "Huey, Lyndon, and Southern Radicalism, Journal of American History, LX (September, 1973), 272; White, Making of the President 1964, p. 357.

[20] Harry Provence, Lyndon B. Johnson: A Biography (New York, 1964), pp. 118-119; Harwood and Johnson, Lyndon, p. 47.

[21] Quoted in Rowland Evans and Robert Novak, Lyndon B. Johnson: The Exercise of Power (New York, 1966), p. 225.

[22] Harwood and Johnson, Lyndon, p. 178.

[23] Sam Houston Johnson, My Brother Lyndon (New York, 1969), p. 193.

[24] Quoted in Wicker, JFK and LBJ, p. 152. The same thought is expressed again by Johnson in The Vantage Point, p. 89.

[25] Quoted in Pool et al, The Formative Years, p. 131.

[26] Harwood and Johnson, Lyndon, p. 47; Williams, "Southern Radicalism," p. 284.

[27] Quoted in Leonard Baker, The Johnson Eclipse: A President's Vice Presidency (New York, 1966), p. 12.

[28] Quoted in Ibid.

[29] David Halberstam, The Best and the Brightest (New York, 1972), p. 450; Baker, The Johnson Eclipse, p. 57.

[30] Davie, LBJ, pp. 62-63.

[31] Quoted in Philip Geyelin, Lyndon B. Johnson and the World (New York, 1966), p. 6.

[32] Harwood and Johnson, Lyndon, p. 52.

[33] Quoted in Theodore H. White, The Making of the President 1968 (New York, 1969), p. 117.

[34] White, Making of the President 1964, p. 55.

[35]Geyelin, Johnson and the World, p. 126.

[36]Quoted in Henry F. Graff, The Tuesday Cabinet: Deliberation and Decision on Peace and War under Lyndon B. Johnson (Englewood Cliffs, 1970), p. 56.

[37]Harwood and Johnson, Lyndon, p. 128.

[38]Davie, LBJ, p. 28.

[39]Halberstam, "Lyndon," p. 75.

[40]Johnson, Vantage Point, p. 95.

[41]White, Making of the President 1964, p. 55.

[42]White, Making of the President 1968, p. 118; Davie, LBJ, p. 8; Halberstam, "Lyndon," p. 75.

[43]White, Making of the President 1964, p. 56; J. Evetts Haley, A Texan Looks at Lyndon: A Study in Illegitimate Power (Canyon, Texas, 1964), pp. 234-235.

[44]Harwood and Johnson, Lyndon, p. 90.

[45]Joseph Kraft, Profiles in Power: A Washington Insight (New York, 1966), p. 10; Williams, "Southern Radicalism," p. 275.

[46]Quoted in Kraft, Profiles in Power, p. 10; Davie, LBJ, p. 8; Alfred Steinberg, Sam Johnson's Boy: A Close-Up of the President From Texas (New York, 1968), p. 740; Halberstam, "Lyndon," pp. 75-76.

[47]Sidey, Personal Presidency, p. 214; Wicker, JFK and LBJ, p. 252.

[48]John J. Pullen, Patriotism in America: A Study of Changing Devotions, 1770-1970 (New York, 1971), p. 20.

[49]Harwood and Johnson, Lyndon, p. 116; Eric F. Goldman, The Tragedy of Lyndon Johnson (New York, 1969), p. 395; Geyelin, Johnson and the World, p. 238.

[50]Quoted in Goldman, Tragedy of Lyndon Johnson, p. 414.

[51]Henry Graff, Tuesday Cabinet, p. 16.

[52]Quoted in Wicker, JFK and LBJ, p. 196.

[53] Quoted in Singer, _Man of Reason_, p. 205.

[54] Quoted in Harwood and Johnson, _Lyndon_, p. 105.

[55] Quoted in Sidey, _Personal Presidency_, p. 22.

[56] _Ibid._, p. 137.

[57] Steinberg, _Sam Johnson's Boy_, pp. 19-20. An excellent minute-by-minute account of the battle of the Alamo can be found in Lon Tinkle, _Thirteen Days to Glory_ (New York, 1958).

[58] Quoted in Pool _et al_, _The Formative Years_, p. 124.

[59] Quoted in Goldman, _Tragedy of Lyndon Johnson_, p. 395.

[60] Quoted in Graff, _Tuesday Cabinet_, p. 104.

[61] George Christian, _The President Steps Down: A Personal Memoir of the Transfer of Power_ (New York, 1970), p. 219; Sidey, _Personal Presidency_, p. 153; White, _Making of the President 1968_, p. 118.

[62] Sidey, _Personal Presidency_, pp. 22-23.

[63] _Ibid._, p. 211.

[64] Quoted in _Ibid._

[65] _Ibid._, p. 213.

[66] Quoted in _Ibid._, p. 212.

[67] _Ibid._, pp. 23; 212; 199.

[68] _Ibid._, p. 199.

[69] Davie, _LBJ_, p. 79.

[70] Sidey, _Personal Presidency_, pp. 153-154.

[71] Booth Mooney, _The Lyndon Johnson Story_ (New York, 1956), pp. 53-55.

[72] Harwood and Johnson, _Lyndon_, pp. 33-35.

[73] Martin Caidin and Edward Hymoff, _The Mission_ (Philadelphia and New York, 1964), p. 22.

[74] _Ibid._, p. 155; Harwood and Johnson, _Lyndon_, p. 35.

[75]Robert Sherrill, The Accidental President (New York, 1967), p. 29; Caidin and Hymoff, The Mission, im passim.

[76]Sherrill, Accidental President, p. 28.

[77]Graff, Tuesday Cabinet, p. 58.

[78]Sherrill, Accidental President, p. 28.

[79]Halberstam, "Lyndon," pp. 79-80.

[80]Quoted in Ibid., p. 80.

[81]Quoted in Graff, Tuesday Cabinet, p. 150.

[82]Halberstam, "Lyndon," p. 79.

[83]Quoted in Ibid.

[84]Halberstam, Best and Brightest, p. 590; Goldman, Tragedy of Lyndon Johnson, p. 522.

[85]Kraft, Profiles in Power, p. 178.

[86]Halberstam, Best and Brightest, pp. 311-315.

[87]Quoted in Ibid., p. 315.

[88]Quoted in Milton Viorst, "Incidentally, who is Dean Rusk?" Esquire, LXIX (April, 1968), 100.

[89]Ibid., p. 99.

[90]Halberstam, Best and Brightest, pp. 553-554; 560.

[91]U.S. National Archives and Records Service, Public Papers of the Presidents of the United States: Lyndon B. Johnson, VII, Doc. 195, April 28, 1967, 470.

[92]Ibid., VII, Doc. 204, May 3, 1967, 497.

[93]Ibid., IX, Doc. 79, February 16, 1968, 234.

[94]Ibid., IX, Doc. 283, May 30, 1968, 673.

[95]Ibid., X, Doc. 384, July 12, 1968, 806.

[96]Townsend Hoopes, The Limits of Intervention: An Inside Account of How the Johnson Policy of Escalation in Vietnam Was Reversed (New York, 1969), pp. 62-65.

[97] Sherrill, Accidental President, p. 220; Provence, Lyndon B. Johnson, p. 115.

[98] Quoted in Sherrill, Accidental President, p. 228.

[99] William S. White, The Professional: Lyndon B. Johnson (Boston, 1964), p. 145.

[100] Ibid.

[101] Geyelin, Johnson and the World, p. 30; Henry A. Zeiger, Lyndon B. Johnson: Man and President (New York, 1963), pp. 34-35; Clarke Newlon, L. B. J. The Man From Johnson City (New York, 1964), pp. 80-81; Mooney, Lyndon Johnson Story, p. 49; White, The Professional, p. 151.

[102] White, The Professional, pp. 168-169; Kraft, Profiles in Power, p. 113.

[103] Halberstam, "Lyndon," p. 86; Steinberg, Sam Johnson's Boy, pp. 372; 375.

[104] Quoted in Steinberg, Sam Johnson's Boy, p. 356.

[105] Zeiger, Man and President, p. 43; Mooney, Lyndon Johnson Story, p. 83.

[106] Quoted in Singer, Man of Reason, p. 195.

[107] Mooney, Lyndon Johnson Story, p. 82.

[108] Zeiger, Man and President, p. 110; Newlon, Man from Johnson City, p. 131; Provence, Lyndon B. Johnson, p. 108.

[109] Johnson, My Brother Lyndon, p. 101.

[110] Quoted in New York Times, January 8, 1958, p. 10.

[111] Ibid., January 9, 1958, p. 32.

[112] Steinberg, Sam Johnson's Boy, p. 581.

[113] Quoted in Ibid., p. 585.

[114] Wicker, JFK and LBJ, pp. 199-203.

[115] Public Papers, I, Doc. 37, December 11, 1963, 43.

[116] Ibid., I, Doc. 119, January 20, 1964, 149.

[117] *Ibid.*, V, Doc. 6, January 12, 1966, 11.

[118] *Ibid.*, VIII, Doc. 485, November 11, 1967, 1020.

[119] *Ibid.*, VIII, Doc. 485, November 11, 1967, 1022.

CONCLUSION

The foregoing pages have attempted to assess the impact of
Lyndon Johnson's Southern heritage, and especially its military
tradition, on his decisions as President. Johnson was not in
any way guilty of beginning the tragic war in Vietnam.
America's involvement with that part of Asia had roots going
back as far as the early 1940's when President Franklin
Roosevelt reacted to Japanese aggression in that region. After
the war, when Vietnamese nationalists waged a struggle to end
French suzerainty over their territory, the Truman and
Eisenhower Administrations took several little-noticed yet still
fateful steps in the direction of increased American commitment
there. And while John F. Kennedy had not instituted large-
scale military support, neither did he do anything to lessen
the United States' role in the war. President Johnson would
inherit a definite commitment to the freedom and independence
of South Vietnam along with his other executive duties.

However, this limited level of American participation in
the Vietnam War would be drastically modified by the new
President. Although running as a peace candidate in the 1964
election, Johnson would soon begin to escalate that war. Month
after month the number of American soldiers in Vietnam increased,
and so did the casualties. Even with the effectiveness of the
war effort in grave doubt, and with his own personal popularity
at shockingly low percentages, President Johnson was nevertheless determined to continue. Finally, in the midst of bitter
dissent throughout the country and within his own party over
the increasingly costly war of attrition, LBJ declined to seek
another term in the White House. A long and distinguished
political career had ended in failure and tragedy.

Among the reasons given for Johnson's behavior as President
was his perception of the lessons of the past. Other Presidents
had fought unpopular wars and there had been many instances of
military interventions without formal Congressional approval in
American history. In like manner, Johnson's own memory of
Fascist aggressions in the 1930's and 1940's had a tremendous
effect upon him. And reinforcing the conceptions he already
held, was the approval and encouragement given by several key
advisers. Yet, probably the most profound influence exerted
on the Chief Executive originated from his Southern heritage.
The South had traditionally been a militant region, a land
characterized by extremely high levels of violent behavior.
Possessing an exaggerated sense of honor and a militant spirit,

114

duels and other forms of personal violence were very common there. But the most prominent trait in this regard had been the great enthusiasm of the South for wars and the military. For various reasons Southerners found the military life very attractive, and the participation of Dixie in America's wars had been conspicuous and glorious. A sacred and self-perpetuating military tradition had become an unmistakable part of the Southern heritage and experience.

It was out of such a heritage that Lyndon Johnson had come. Deeply impressed with the history of his family and his region, he was proud of his Southern background. But while a source of pride, it was also one of pain and frustration for him because of the large amount of regional prejudice exhibited toward his section by outsiders. Being typically Southern in manners and speech, he always felt that many people looked down upon him because of his background. The most crucial of his Southern traits, however, was his great respect for the military. His legislative career had been closely connected with military affairs, and this did not change when he became President. Holding the attitudes so characteristic of the Southern military tradition, he engaged the nation in its most unpopular war, and divided his country bitterly over the issue of that conflict.

In assessing this President from the South, it must be admitted that few men holding that office before him had passed so many visionary ideas and hopes into actual law. His performance in domestic affairs during the early part of his Presidency was nothing short of brilliant, and gave him his chance for greatness and a place of honor beside his beloved F. D. R. in the annals of history. But fate was to dictate otherwise. Lyndon Johnson's opportunity for greatness fell a casualty to the fighting in the far-off jungles of Southeast Asia, while at home cities were decaying, race riots were raging, and pollution was spreading. Lyndon's legacy would be the memory of a stubborn and unbending man intoxicated by his role of Commander-in-Chief, and an era of violence, confusion, and national frustration. In thinking fondly about the return to private life, Johnson was most concerned about the South, about "the cost of my program to 11 states and 22 men," an obvious reference to the eleven original states of the Confederacy and their senators. Looking back on a lifetime of enormous labors, he could calmly say: "I am well satisfied." But his country was not satisfied, and when he did retire his fellow Americans repudiated and reviled him with almost unprecedented intensity.[1]

Although he had been responsible for great accomplishments, his ego outstripped his achievements, and his personality embittered those whom he most wanted to please. While there

are occasions when retreat is wiser than attack, and when
acknowledgement of error is more brave than persistence in it,
Lyndon Johnson found such notions absurd and incomprehensible.
The country's tragedy was that LBJ instinctively equated
national prestige with his own, because as the war dragged on
and on, there was an ever-growing suspicion that there was a
larger concern with American pride than with Vietnamese welfare.
Johnson was from the South, and he had been deeply imbued with
the myth of American invincibility, the legend that the United
States will always prevail in the end. And pride was a factor.
How could Lyndon Baines Johnson, overwhelmingly elected President
of the United States, ever doubt that his nation--the mightiest
nation in the world, with an unbroken string of military
successes--could lick a rag-tag bunch of poorly equipped
guerrilla soldiers in a tiny and undeveloped country in Asia?[2]

The President from Texas was also in many ways a prisoner
of the past. Past history can be neatly arranged and set down
in orderly pages of dates and episodes. But history as it
occurs is an amorphous and unpredictable phenomenon, not
nearly so amenable to comfortable generalization. A grasp and
understanding of history as it happens depends much more
heavily upon the intuitions of leaders, leaders who must sometimes be willing to make a break with the events of the past,
who must on occasion throw away outworn ideas. The leader, too,
must be capable of explaining the history he is making to an
increasingly better educated citizenry whose life span has
already encountered rapid change of the most sweeping magnitude.
It so happened that Johnson was leading at a time when the old
values were changing; there were new forces at work, and many
time-honored institutions of society and government were being
severely challenged and tested. And it was also his fate to
preside at a time when an unpopular and complex war was being
covered in more detail by the mass media than any other conflict
in American history.[3]

In this same regard, Johnson emphasized too much the handi-
cap of his Southern origin. He was certainly correct in sensing
that his Southernism had engendered distrust and scorn, and
had helped to obscure many people's view of him. Yet, that was
not the sole reason. Because in many ways he was a stranger
in the America of the 1960's. It is true that his Southern
heritage had something to do with his alienation, because he
had been raised in the South and he clearly carried that region
distinctive manner with him, and some did mock and ridicule
him because of it. There was, however, more to the estrangement
than that. Instead, it consisted of many factors, a large
proportion of which can be placed under the general category of
"generational." Johnson was a product of the age of the Great
Depression and the time of the Fascist dictators. He brought
into the decade of the 1960's the values gained from that

116

earlier period, only to find that a new generation was re-
jecting many of those values. Not only did the generation of
young people in college not remember the Depression years,
they had also been born after World War II and after the
beginnings of the Cold War, and to them the conflict in Vietnam
made no sense at all. Johnson was an alien in the new America,
an individual whose manner and very physique defied the modern
standards and styles. He was a gaudy and flamboyant man with
the background and the values of the Southern frontier,
wandering uncomfortably among the hip "Pepsi generation." He
was a master at manipulating people; they demanded that every-
body "do his own thing." He believed in institutions like
government, business, and universities; they were constantly
attacking them. He was a paternalist; they valued permissive-
ness. He believed in heroes; theirs was the age of the non-
hero. He extolled patriotism and strength; they understood
those words in a very different context.[4]

And finally, if history had caught up with Lyndon Johnson,
then irony had caught up with American history. Because in
that critical hour of the nation's experience, when John
Kennedy was dead and the war in Vietnam could be continued or
ended, history had ironically placed two living exponents of
the Southern military tradition into positions of the greatest
delicacy and power. A man from Texas was in the White House
and a man from Georgia was in the State Department, and both
gentlemen came with a renewed allegiance and dedication to the
national myths of innocence and invincibility.[5] But the
cruelest irony was reserved for Lyndon Johnson himself, an
unusually gifted President who just happened to be, in the words
of Eric Goldman, "the wrong man from the wrong place at the
wrong time under the wrong circumstances."[6] Yet, in the final
analysis, all the tragedy and heartbreak of Vietnam cannot be
blamed entirely on Lyndon Johnson and the South. Because the
South was American a long time before it ever became uniquely
or self-consciously Southern. And if indeed, as several writers
have suggested, many Southern characteristics are merely
American traits modified and exaggerated, then all Americans
have occasion for reflection.[7]

CONCLUSION

FOOTNOTES

[1]Theodore H. White, The Making of the President 1968
(New York, 1969), p. 111; Alfred Steinberg, Sam Johnson's Boy:
A Close-Up of the President From Texas (New York, 1968),
p. 696; Henry F. Graff, The Tuesday Cabinet: Deliberation and
Decision on Peace and War under Lyndon B. Johnson (Englewood
Cliffs, 1970), p. 173; Richard Harwood and Haynes Johnson,
Lyndon (New York, 1973), p. 144.

[2]White, Making of the President 1968, pp. 506-507; Tom
Wicker, JFK and LBJ: The Influence of Personality Upon Politics
(New York, 1968), pp. 207; 251-252; Townsend Hoopes, The Limits
of Intervention: An Inside Account of How the Johnson Policy
of Escalation in Vietnam Was Reversed (New York, 1969),
p. 240; C. Vann Woodward, The Burden of Southern History,
Revised edition (New York, 1968), p. 154.

[3]White, Making of the President 1968, p. 112; Harwood
and Johnson, Lyndon, p. 182; Chester L. Cooper, The Lost
Crusade: America in Vietnam (New York, 1970), p. 412.

[4]T. Harry Williams, "Huey, Lyndon, and Southern
Radicalism," Journal of American History, LX (September, 1973),
291-292; John J. Pullen, Patriotism in America: A Study of
Changing Devotions, 1770-1970, (New York, 1971), p. 123.

[5]Woodward, Burden of Southern History, pp. 160-161.

[6]Eric F. Goldman, The Tragedy of Lyndon Johnson (New York,
1969), p. 531.

[7]Howard Zinn, The Southern Mystique (New York, 1970),
pp. 218; 238-263; W. J. Cash, The Mind of the South (New York,
1941), p. xx; Woodward, Burden of Southern History, p. 31.

BIBLIOGRAPHY

Alden, John Richard. The South in the Revolution, 1763-1789. Baton Rouge: Louisiana State University Press, 1957.

Ashmore, Harry S. An Epitaph for Dixie. New York: W. W. Norton and Company, 1957.

Baker, Leonard. The Johnson Eclipse: A President's Vice Presidency. New York: The Macmillan Company, 1966.

Bell, Jack. The Johnson Treatment: How Lyndon B. Johnson Took Over the Presidency and Made It His Own. New York: Harper & Row, 1965.

Bertelson, David. The Lazy South. New York: Oxford University Press, 1967.

Bonner, James C. "The Historical Basis of Southern Military Tradition," The Georgia Review, IX (1955), 74-85.

Brearley, H. C. "The Pattern of Violence," in Culture in the South. Edited by W. T. Couch. Chapel Hill: University of North Carolina Press, 1934.

Buck, Paul H. The Road to Reunion: 1865-1900. Boston: Little Brown and Company, 1937.

Carpenter, Jesse T. The South as a Conscious Minority, 1789-1861: A Study in Political Thought. New York: New York University Press, 1930.

Carter, Hodding. Southern Legacy. Baton Rouge: Louisiana State University Press, 1950.

Cash, W. J. The Mind of the South. New York: Alfred A. Knopf, 1941.

Christian, George. The President Steps Down: A Personal Memoir of the Transfer of Power. New York: Macmillan Company, 1970.

Caidin, Martin and Edward Hymoff. The Mission. Philadelphia and New York: J. B. Lippincott Company, 1964.

Cooper, Chester L. The Lost Crusade: America in Vietnam. New York: Dodd, Mead & Company, 1970.

Coulter, E. Merton. The Confederate States of America, 1861-1865. Baton Rouge: Louisiana State University Press, 1950.

Current, Richard N. Lincoln and the First Shot. Philadelphia and New York: J. B. Lippincott Company, 1963.

Dabbs, James McBride. The Southern Heritage. New York: Alfred A. Knopf, 1959.

Davie, Michael. LBJ: A Foreign Observer's Viewpoint. New York: Duell, Sloan and Pearce, 1966.

Eaton, Clement. A History of the Old South. 2nd ed. New York: Macmillan Company, 1966.

Evans, Rowland and Robert Novak. Lyndon B. Johnson: The Exercise of Power. New York: New American Library, 1966.

Ezell, John Samuel. The South Since 1865. New York: Macmillan Company, 1963.

"The Fighting South." Life, XIII (1942), 57-71.

Franklin, John Hope. The Militant South: 1800-1861. Cambridge: Harvard University Press, 1956.

_____. "The North, the South, and the American Revolution," Journal of American History, LXII (1975), 5-23.

Gaston, Paul M. The New South Creed: A Study in Southern Mythmaking. New York: Alfred A. Knopf, 1970.

Geyelin, Philip. Lyndon B. Johnson and the World. New York: Frederick A. Praeger, 1966.

Goldman, Eric F. The Tragedy of Lyndon Johnson. New York: Alfred A. Knopf, 1969.

Graff, Henry F. The Tuesday Cabinet: Deliberation and Decision on Peace and War under Lyndon B. Johnson. Englewood Cliffs: Prentice-Hall, Inc., 1970.

Graves, John Temple. The Fighting South. New York: G. P. Putnam's Sons, 1943.

Hackney, Sheldon. "Southern Violence," The American Historical Review, LXXIV (1969), 906-925.

Halberstam, David. The Best and the Brightest. New York: Random House, 1972.

_____. "Lyndon," Esquire, LXXVIII (1972), 73-88.

Haley, J. Evetts. A Texan Looks at Lyndon: A Study in Illegitimate Power. Canyon, Texas: Palo Duro Press, 1964.

Harwood, Richard and Haynes Johnson. Lyndon. New York: Praeger Publishers, 1973.

Hesseltine, William B. and David L. Smiley. The South in American History. 2nd ed. Englewood Cliffs, Prentice-Hall, Inc., 1960.

Hoopes, Townsend. The Limits of Intervention: An Inside Account of How the Johnson Policy of Escalation in Vietnam Was Reversed. New York: David McKay Company, 1969.

Johnson, Lyndon Baines. The Vantage Point: Perspectives of the Presidency, 1963-1969. New York: Holt, Rinehart and Winston, 1971.

Johnson, Sam Houston. My Brother Lyndon. Edited by Enrique Hank Lopez. New York: Cowles Book Company, Inc., 1969.

Kluckhohn, Frank L. Lyndon's Legacy: A Candid Look at the President's Policymakers. New York: Davin-Adair Company, 1964.

Kraft, Joseph. Profiles in Power: A Washington Insight. New York: New American Library, Inc., 1966.

"Life Visits Audie Murphy." Life, XIX (1945), 94-97.

McPherson, Harry. A Political Education. Boston: Little, Brown and Company, 1972.

Meade, Robert Douthat. "The Military Spirit of the South," Current History, XXX (1929), 55-60.

Mooney, Booth. The Lyndon Johnson Story. New York: Farrar. Straus and Cudahy, 1956.

Newlon, Clarke. L. B. J. The Man from Johnson City. New York: Dodd, Mead & Company, 1964.

New York Times. 1958; 1963.

_____. The Pentagon Papers. New York: Bantam Books, Inc., 1971.

Osterweis, Rollin G. The Myth of the Lost Cause. Hamden, Conn: The Shoe String Press, Inc., 1973.

_____. Romanticism and Nationalism in the Old South. New Haven: Yale University Press, 1949.

Pool, William C., Emmie Craddock and David E. Conrad. Lyndon Baines Johnson: The Formative Years. San Marcos: Southwest Texas College Press, 1965.

Provence, Harry. Lyndon B. Johnson: A Biography. New York: Fleet Publishing Corporation, 1964.

Pullen, John J. Patriotism in America: A Study of Changing Devotions, 1770-1970. New York: American Heritage Press, 1971.

Roberts, Charles. LBJ's Inner Circle. New York: Delacorte Press, 1965.

Schlesinger, Arthur M., Jr. A Thousand Days: John F. Kennedy in the White House. Boston: Houghton Mifflin Company, 1965.

_____. The Bitter Heritage: Vietnam and American Democracy 1941-1966. Boston: Houghton Mifflin Company, 1966.

_____. Violence: America in the Sixties. New York: New American Library, 1968.

Sherrill, Robert. The Accidental President. New York: Grossman Publishers, 1967.

Sidey, Hugh. A Very Personal Presidency: Lyndon Johnson in the White House. New York: Atheneum, 1968.

Simkins, Francis Butler and Charles Pierce Roland. A History of the South. 4th ed. New York: Alfred A. Knopf, 1972.

Singer, Kurt and Jane Sherrod. Lyndon Baines Johnson, Man of Reason. Minneapolis: T. S. Denison & Company, 1964.

Steinberg, Alfred. Sam Johnson's Boy: A Close-Up of the President From Texas. New York: Macmillan Company, 1968.

Tindall, George Brown. *The Emergence of the New South, 1913-1945.* Baton Rouge: Louisiana State University Press, 1967.

Tinkle, Lon. *Thirteen Days to Glory.* New York: McGraw-Hill, 1958.

U. S. National Archives and Records Service. *Public Papers of the Presidents of the United States: Lyndon B. Johnson.* 10 vols. Washington: Government Printing Office, 1964-69.

Vandiver, Frank. "The Southerner as Extremist," in *The Idea of the South.* Edited by Frank Vandiver. Chicago: University of Chicago Press, 1964.

Viorst, Milton. "Incidentally, who is Dean Rusk?" *Esquire,* LXIX (1968), 99-181.

Watters, Pat. *The South and the Nation.* New York: Pantheon Books, 1969.

Webb, Walter Prescott. *The Great Plains.* Boston: Ginn and Company, 1931.

White, Theodore H. *The Making of the President 1964.* New York: Atheneum Publishers, 1965.

_____. *The Making of the President 1968.* New York: Atheneum Publishers, 1969.

White, William S. *The Professional: Lyndon B. Johnson.* Boston: Houghton Mifflin Company, 1964.

Wicker, Tom. *JFK and LBJ: The Influence of Personality Upon Politics.* New York: William Morrow & Company, 1968.

Williams, T. Harry. "Huey, Lyndon, and Southern Radicalism," *Journal of American History,* LX (1973), 267-293.

Williams, William Appleman. "Ol Lyndon," *New York Review of Books,* XVII (1971), 3-6.

Woodward, C. Vann. *The Burden of Southern History.* Revised edition. New York: New American Library, 1968.

Zeiger, Henry A. *Lyndon B. Johnson: Man and President.* New York: Popular Library, 1963.

Zinn, Howard. *The Southern Mystique.* New York: Alfred A. Knopf, 1970.